50 Ways to Cope with your Child's Death

A Guide for Grieving Parents

OTHER BOOKS OF INTEREST FROM MARQUETTE BOOKS

John Wheeler, *Last Man Out: Memoirs of the Last Associated Press Reporter Castro Kicked Out of Cuba in the 1960s* (forthcoming 2008). ISBN: 978-0-922993-84-0

Steve Hallock, *War Stories from Great American Journalists of the Late 20th Century* (forthcoming 2008). ISBN: 978-0-922993-85-7

Eric G. Stephan and R. Wayne Pace, *Seven Secrets of Successful, Happy People* (2008). ISBN 978-0-922993-75-8

Dan Robison, *Death Chant: Kimo's Battle with the Shamanic Forces* (2006). ISBN: 0-922993-52-1

Phillip J. Tichenor, *Athena's Forum: A Historical Novel* (2005). ISBN: 0-922993-27-0

Melvin DeFleur, *A Return to Innocence: A Novel* (2005). ISBN: 0-922993-50-5

Dan Robison, *Wind Seer: The Story of One Native American Boy's Contribution to the Anasazi Culture* (2005). ISBN: 0-922993-27-0

Ray Edwards, *Justice Never Sleeps: A Novel of Murder and Revenge in Spokane* (2005). ISBN: 0-922993-26-2

John M. Burke, *From Prairie to Palace: The Lost Biography of Buffalo Bill* (2005). ISBN: 0-922993-21-1

Dan Robison, *Kimo's Escape: The Story of a Hawaiian Boy Who Learns to Believe in Himself* (2005). ISBN: 0-922993-28-9

Tonya Holmes Shook, *The Drifters: A Christian Historical Novel about the Melungeon Shantyboat People* (2005). ISBN: 0-922993-19-X

David Demers, *China Girl: One Man's Adoption Story* (2004). ISBN: 0-922993-08-4

50 Ways to Cope with your Child's Death

A Guide for Grieving Parents

Norma Sawyers-Kurz

Marquette Books
Spokane, Washington

Copyright © 2008 by Marquette Books

All rights reserved. No part of this publication may be reproduced, stored in a retrieval system, or transmitted in any form or by any means, electronic, mechanical, photocopying, microfilming, recording, or otherwise, without permission of the publisher.

Printed in the United States of America on acid-free paper.

Library of Congress Cataloging-in-Publication Data

Sawyers-Kurz, Norma, 1943-
50 ways to cope with your child's death : a guide for grieving parents / Norma Sawyers-Kurz.
p. cm.
Includes bibliographical references and index.
ISBN 978-0-922993-24-6 (pbk. : alk. paper)
1. Grief. 2. Children--Death. 3. Parents--Psychology.
4. Adjustment (Psychology) I. Title.
BF575.G7S29 2008
155.9'37--dc22

2007035670

Cover photograph Copyright © Chris Vervaeke,
Courtesy of Fotolia.com

Marquette Books LLC
3107 East 62nd Avenue
Spokane, Washington 99223
509-443-7057 (voice) / 509-448-2191 (fax)
books@marquettebooks.com / www.MarquetteBooks.com

Dedication

To Neal, Hunter, and Landon,
my three grandsons, who have been
a great blessing in my life

Lilies of the Valley

"*Return to Happiness*"

Contents

Introduction 9
1 Coping with Shock and Denial 19
2 Coping with Emotions & Loneliness 31
3 Coping with Depression 39
4 Coping with Panic 51
5 Coping with Guilt 59
6 Coping with Anger 69
7 Coping with Physical Aspects of Grief 77
8 Coping with Life Changes 85
9 Engaging in Meaningful Activity 97
10 Affirming Reality 107
Final Comment 113
Web Site Resources 115
Bibliography 117
Index 121

Introduction

I had just finished with a customer at my beauty salon when one of my daughter's friends came running into the shop, screaming that Karen had been involved in a motor-vehicle accident.

Lewis, my husband, was next door at his barber shop and also had just gotten the news. We both ran into the street toward the scene of the accident, which was one block away. Someone tried to restrain me when I got to the scene, but I broke away. I had to see my daughter, who was lying unconscious on the street. Her eyes were fixed, staring, as bystanders were administering cardiopulmonary resuscitation to her still body.

It was March 5, 1982. Karen was only fifteen. She had been riding on the back of a motorcycle driven by a friend. She was going to cut his hair. They were riding from school to our businesses when a truck struck them at an intersection. The impact threw both of them toward a car waiting at a stop sign. Karen's helmet came off, and her head struck the pavement. The boy's helmet remained intact. He suffered a severe concussion and multiple fractures but later recovered completely.

Glancing at Lewis, I saw terror on his face. He began crying and moaning, "She's gone! She's gone!"

I don't believe it, I thought. *It's not true! Karen would be all right. My daughter and I were fighters. I would stay by her side until she recovered. She would be all right.*

In a stupor, I watched as she continued to receive first aid. *This is unreal,* I kept thinking. *Any moment now I will wake up and find this to be a bad dream.*

A large, quiet group of bystanders—friends and relatives—gathered around us. Our 16-year-old son, David, had come upon the scene and now was standing with his head leaned against a parked truck. He was sobbing, shaking. My heart cried out to him and my husband. But I was numb—too numb to even cry.

As we waited for the ambulance to arrive, time seemed to stand still. *What is taking them so long? Don't they know my daughter could be dying?* Finally, the ambulance arrived and the medical attendants transported our daughter to a small, nearby hospital. I rode in the ambulance. Lewis and David took our car as we all headed for the medical facility.

Again and again, I tried to convince myself that Karen was going to be all right. Yet I was frightened. My mouth became so dry that my tongue felt like cotton. I watched as the paramedics worked on my daughter. *Just keep at it. Keep working with her. She'll come through.*

The ride to the hospital seemed to take forever, but at last we arrived. Breathing heavily, I followed the attendants as they rushed Karen into the building. After a short period of time, a doctor came to inform us that Karen's condition was critical, and she was to be transferred to larger hospital facilities in another city.

We followed the ambulance transporting our daughter to the hospital until mechanical problems with our car forced us to finish the trip with relatives. The ride seemed endless. Karen was in the ambulance, and we had no idea what was happening to her. We didn't even know if she was still alive. Lewis' brother and sister-in-law tried to comfort us during the trip. We sat silently in the back seat. Our thoughts and our feelings could not be turned into words.

After arriving at the hospital, we were taken to a room to wait for the doctor's report. A short time later a physician came to give us his prognosis. He said Karen was in a deep coma from the severe head injury, not breathing on her own, and unresponsive to all stimuli. She was "clinically silent."

Head scans had been taken, and they were flat. More scans would be performed later to see if there was any change, but the outlook wasn't good. We were informed that machines were sustaining our daughter's life. Drugs administered through her veins were keeping her heart beating and maintaining her blood pressure, and a respirator was pumping oxygen into her lungs.

The doctor was trying to gently tell us Karen'scondition was terminal, but I couldn't accept that prognosis. My heart could not hear him. Staring at me strangely, the doctor asked, "Do you understand what I am saying, Mrs. Sawyers?" Although I could hear myself answering, "Yes," I found it difficult to believe I was actually speaking. How could I utter a word that seemed to signify the collapse of my family's world?

Many of Karen's friends joined us at the hospital to await news of her condition, and we were glad they were there for support. That evening and the following days were a blur of faces and embraces as our family and our friends sought to comfort us.

As we waited, I was haunted with many questions. *Why had this senseless calamity befallen our little one? Why did it have to be Karen? It wasn't fair! Karen was so beautiful—her life so full of hope and promise. Why was life being stolen from her just as she was beginning to blossom and to taste life's joys?*

The three of us were finally allowed into Intensive Care to see Karen. My daughter's chest moved up and down as the mechanical respirator breathed for her. She was completely still. Her eyes were partially open and staring.

A nurse explained that everything possible was being done for our daughter. I took my daughter's hand and softly spoke to her. "I love you Karen. We all love you." We all spoke loving words as if she were listening. But there was no response. She seemed lifeless, withdrawn.

As we continued the vigil, more questions tortured me. *Does she know what's going on? What if she is suffering and can't tell me?* Oh, how could we bear this torment? I wished to be home so I could just run down the road and scream. *Would it help to do that? Where was my help? What was my help?*

On Saturday we conferred again with the neurologist. "I'm sorry to have to tell you that the head scan shows no improvement," he reported. "The readings are flat. Another brain scan will be taken tomorrow to see if there is any change. If there is no change, after the period of time required by law, your daughter should be taken off the machines maintaining life functions. To leave her on the life-supporting machines would only prolong her present condition artificially. Medically we have done all we can. We don't expect you to make the decision. After the prescribed period of time has passed, we will decide."

That evening, in the waiting room, we managed to get a little sleep. But I woke often and went through the list of "if-onlys.' *If only I had told Karen that she couldn't cut the boy's hair—If only I had not given her permission to ride on the boy's motorcycle—If only I could turn back the clock and make this stop ...*

We had always been so careful with our children, never taking chances on their health or safety. When they were sick, we immediately took them to visit the doctor. Once David had broken his foot, and Karen had hurt her knee in sports. We took both to specialists where they received the finest care. Now—after all the years of care and concern—this horrible tragedy.

Two days had passed since our daughter's tragic accident. It was Sunday morning, March 7, 1982. That morning Karen's physicians informed us there was no hope for her recovery. It was apparent to them that our daughter's brain had been irreversibly damaged. Karen had lost her higher brain functions—she could no longer think, she could no longer feel. In other words, Karen was no longer Karen. And, the doctors said, Karen never would be again.

We knew Karen wouldn't want such a condition to continue. The feisty, fun-loving girl we had known and loved for fifteen years would not want any part of that sort of helpless existence. For Karen's sake, the doctors felt that the best thing to do was to cease artificial life-support. Further treatment was hopeless. We had to let go of Karen. We had to let our precious daughter die in peace.

As I awoke the following morning, the realization that my daughter was gone washed over me like a tidal wave of grief. Despair engulfed me. From that moment, each day meant facing the paradox of the unfaceable. Across the bed and in the next room, I knew my husband and my son were experiencing their own profound grief.

In the mournful days, weeks, and months right after her accident and death, I was an emotional basket case, nearly paralyzed by my suffering. It took extreme effort for me to function even at the simplest level. At home, my legs dragged as I mechanically went through the motions of cooking, cleaning, and laundry washing.

At my beauty salon business, apprehension filled me each morning as I thought of facing my tasks. From the moment I had seen Karen lying unconscious on the street after her accident, I had difficulty communicating with others. It was difficult for me at work because I was experiencing so much trouble concentrating. My customers went out of their way to offer me sympathy, and I couldn't have survived without their support, yet it was hard during those days for me to appear interested and attentive in what was occurring around me. As customers chatted with me, I hoped I was nodding at the correct times and saying the right things. I wasn't very good company.

I couldn't seem to escape from my sorrow. I found it impossible to become absorbed in a book or in television because my attention span had become so short. Feeling disassociated from my surroundings and from the concerns of the world, I found it difficult to socialize with family or friends. Food no longer attracted me because now my appetite was gone; it was difficult for me to even consume an entire sandwich. While other people were on diets to lose weight, I was losing weight without even trying. Sleep wasn't an escape either. I intermittently woke up with a start, with an empty feeling in the pit of my stomach. Day and night, the realization of the loss of my daughter weighed heavily upon me.

In my worst moments, I panicked. I worried that the quicksand of my grief would pull me down farther and farther down until I lost my mind. I longed to flee, to somehow escape from the pain of my grief. But life did not spare me. There was no way to disengage from the suffering. And, the fact is, I did want to live. I knew my remaining family, whom I deeply loved and cared about, needed me. What I wanted most then was to somehow incorporate this terrible loss into my life so I could become a whole person again. It was tough, and it took many years of struggle, but with the support of others and my faith in God, I succeeded in rebuilding my life. I was able to meet my daughter's death on its own anguishing terms, grieve over it, ask questions, and in time allow it to become a part of my life's complex pattern.

Competent doctors and psychiatrists have written many books about the grieving process. I encourage you to read them. What makes this book unique is that it is written by someone who has experienced what you are now experiencing — the loss of a child.

In the pages that follow, I will try to help you understand what is happening to you and will provide you with appropriate ways for coping with grief so that you, too, can rebuild your life as I have. At this point, you may not feel that you can overcome your child's death. You may feel, like I once did, that there is no escape from grief. Yet I escaped. It didn't happen overnight. It took many years of prayer and interaction with family, friends and professionals to cope with the death of my daughter.

But I survived and, in this book, I will share with you some of the ways in which you, too, can cope with and survive your own child's death. The 50 suggestions provided in this book are drawn from my own personal experience as well as from the expertise of many doctors, professors and others who have studied the grieving process. They are organized into 10 chapters that roughly parallel what experts call the stages of grieving:

Introduction

1. COPING WITH SHOCK AND DENIAL
2. COPING WITH EMOTIONS & LONELINESS
3. COPING WITH DEPRESSION
4. COPING WITH PANIC
5. COPING WITH GUILT
6. COPING WITH ANGER
7. COPING WITH PHYSICAL ASPECTS OF GRIEF
8. COPING WITH LIFE CHANGES
9. ENGAGING IN MEANINGFUL ACTIVITY
10. AFFIRMING REALITY

Of course, I cannot guarantee that reading this book will help everyone. But I hope some of the suggestions provide comfort to you and help heal your soul.

Norma Sawyers-Kurz
Fall 2007

Chapter 1

Coping with Shock and Denial

When your child dies, you can feel as if your whole life has been shattered and nothing will ever be the same. Whether your loss came unexpectedly or after a long-term illness, you and your family are likely to experience shock and denial, according to experts on death and dying. You will find it difficult to accept the fact that it happened.

Such sorrow, experts say, often "anesthetizes" us, preventing us from having to face the grim reality all at once. In other words, we know intellectually that our child has died, but emotionally we don't want to believe it, so unconsciously we set barriers in the way, making complete acceptance a slow process. Shock and denial give us time to accustom ourselves to the terrible facts.

The shock-and-denial stage may last anywhere from a few minutes or hours to a few days or weeks.[1] But it happens to most people. And contrary to popular belief, this stage is a good thing. It offers a temporary mental escape that sustains us until we are emotionally ready to move on to the next stage of grief.

1. Ask for Assistance in Dealing with Details Such as Funeral Arrangements

When we are numb with shock, everyday activities of life can seem like enormous tasks. It can take all of our strength, for example, just to take care of our physical needs, such as food preparation and grooming. More complex tasks, like making funeral arrangements, are even more daunting.

In *Surviving Grief and Learning to Live Again*, Catherine M. Sanders, a psychologist specializing in bereavement, notes that "the rituals of death require a lot from us, not the least of which is that first awful, wrenching trip to the funeral home to make the arrangements."[2] She adds that at a time when we feel least prepared for decision making, we are bombarded with numerous questions, leaving us feeling overwhelmed.

---

[1] See Granger E. Westberg, *Good Grief: A Constructive Approach to the Problem of Loss* (Minneapolis: Augsburg Fortress Press, 1979) for an excellent listing of the stages of grief.
[2] Catherine M. Sanders, *Surviving Grief and Learning to Live Again* (New York: John Wiley and Sons, Inc, 1992), p. 48.

If you find that taking care of these responsibilities or even thinking clearly is difficult, enlist the assistance of friends or relatives. Most of the people closest to you would like to lend a hand, so let them know how they can aid you during this extremely difficult early period. Perhaps you need assistance for such tasks as writing the obituary, answering the phone, preparing the meals, and so worth. Don't be ashamed to ask or receive much needed help with these tasks.

2. Accept Emotional Support from Friends, Relatives, and Other Parents

The heartache and pain associated with losing your child is so traumatic that just getting up in the morning to face the day can be a challenge.

To help you through this process, accept emotional support from friends and relatives. In addition to loyalty, they provide love and sympathy and can help you share the pain. Talk to them.

Don't be disappointed, however, if some friends or relatives don't know what to say. People often have difficulty expressing themselves well or reaching out to each other during times of grief. Some people will lift you up with their encouraging words. Others have more difficulty expressing their support. In addition, be aware that some friends or relatives may avoid you during this time or refuse to talk about the tragedy for fear that it may bring either you or them too much grief.

Other parents who have lost a child can be another source of emotional support. Of course, your loss is unique, so no one else can say that they know exactly how you feel or what you are going through. But other parents who have experienced a loss are in a better position to understand what you are going through. Seek them out and share your story with them.

In fact, you may want to join a support group of other parents who have lost children. In *How to Go on Living When Someone You Love Dies,* bereavement specialist Therese A. Rando writes that "self-help groups can be wonderfully therapeutic in assisting you with your mourning."[3] She writes that support groups not only provide us with encouragement, they also provide practical suggestions for dealing with grief. These groups can help fill a gap when we find that others avoid us.[4]

Don't expect that any one person will have all the insight and compassion you crave. But do accept whatever emotional support you can from those who have experienced the loss of a child.

3. Seek Guidance from
A Minister or Skilled Counselor

In his book *Healing Your Grieving Heart: 100 Practical Ideas,* Alan D. Wolfelt says that "while grief

---

[3]Therese A. Rando, *How to Go on Living When Someone You Love Dies* (New York: Bantam Books, 1991), p. 311.

[4]For additional information on support groups, including some Web sites, refer to No. 18 in Chapter 3.

counseling is not for everyone, many individuals are helped through their grief journeys by a compassionate counselor."[5] He advises that, if possible, you should locate a counselor experienced in dealing with grief and loss issues. He adds that your pastor or spiritual leader also may be a good source of counsel at this time, but only if he or she understands your needs to mourn your loss and to search for meaning.

This doesn't mean that parents who lose a child shouldn't talk to friends or relatives. But a pastor or counselor usually has more knowledge and resources to help you work through emotions like anger and guilt. They also can validate your loss and provide a frame of reference as to what constitutes "healthy" mourning. Some people also prefer the safety and security of a therapeutic environment.

The choice of counselor will depend upon your needs. If you desire counseling from a religious perspective, seek out a member of the clergy. But some secular counselors, psychologists and psychiatrists also understand the importance of spirituality and have been trained to provide emotional as well as spiritual guidance.

In addition to ministers and psychologists, other resources include crisis centers that focus on coping with tragedy and sorrow and, as noted above, bereavement groups that help people work through the grief process.

---

[5] Alan D. Wolfelt, *Healing Your Grieving Heart: 100 Practical Ideas* (Fort Collins, CO: Companion Press, 1998), p. 67.

4. Write Your Feelings in a Journal

Writing is another way of releasing emotions during the early stages of grief. You can begin by attempting to answer the questions you have been asking yourself over and over again. "Why did this happen?" "How can I go on?"

You also may have feelings or thoughts you wish you had shared with your child while he or she was still alive. Write a letter in your journal to your child. Pour out your heart. Express your love and say all the things you wish you had said.

Identify any unfinished business or unresolved emotional issues in the relationship with your child, and then write down the words you wish you had said. "I love you," or "I'm sorry," or "I needed you."

Rando says that "although you cannot have the actual interaction with your loved one ... there are ways that you can deal with unfinished business. ... Sometimes writing a letter to your lost loved one can be therapeutic."[6]

Of course, you may also question your faith or your religion. Don't be afraid to express yourself and talk with others.

---

[6]Rando, *How to Go on Living When Someone You Love Dies*, p. 252.

5. Be Gentle and Kind to Yourself

If you're like most people who lose a child, you are probably wondering how you will ever learn to go on with the rest of your life. But with the support of family and friends and perhaps God (if you are spiritual), you can nurture yourself into believing once again in your life.

Note that I said "nurture," because overcoming grief doesn't happen in days, weeks, or even months. It usually takes years for many parents to integrate the death of a child into the fabric of their lives.

Pay close attention to your emotional and physical well-being.[7] You are emotionally vulnerable right now, so don't beat yourself up for any action, deed, or word from the past. The past is gone, so the best thing to do now is to focus on the future and on your eventual recovery.

Concentrate on your physical well-being as well. When grief is intense, the body uses up vast amounts of emotional and physical energy. Nancy O'Connor, author of *Letting Go With Love: The Grieving Process*, says we should go easy on ourselves during early grief, because "mental confusion and low energy levels are very common. Fatigue and exhaustion result from both expending the energy to cope and resisting the emotional responses that continue to surface."[8]

---

[7] See Chapters 2 and 7 in this book for more details about taking care of your health.

[8] Nancy O'Connor, *Letting Go With Love: The Grieving Process* (Tucson, AZ: La Mariposa Press, 1984), p. 19.

It is vitally important at this time for you to get proper nutrition and the best rest you can. Don't overdo it. Your most special need right now is to be gentle and kind to yourself.

6. Carry on with Normal Activities as Much as Possible

It is good for us to keep fairly busy with our usual daily activities during the first stage of grief. Although we may need help with some tasks early on, it is certainly not good to become completely dependent on others or to let them make all our decisions for us. There is therapeutic value in doing things for ourselves, because this will help most of us come out of the shock phase and move us into the grief process.

Staying busy is good because it also helps prevent us from dwelling too much on painful memories. In her book, *How to Survive the Loss of a Child,* Sanders says that "the search for some meaning in a child's death is an ongoing rumination for survivors. It is as if we must unearth every detail surrounding the death, so we can begin to piece together this incomprehensible tragedy."[9]

Intense thinking about the circumstances surrounding the death of a child is a natural response to the loss and a reflection of the internal grief. However, preoccupation with thoughts about our child's death can

---

[9]*Catherine M. Sanders, How to Survive the Loss of a Child* (New York: Three Rivers Press, 1998), p. 17.

become obsessive. Mental images can run through our minds until they seem like a flood that can't be stopped. We can mentally ponder over details regarding aspects of our loss until we feel overwhelmed. At those times, when our minds are running in circles, there are some steps we can take to fix our minds on more pleasant thoughts.

First, we can recognize that memories can seem more profound in certain situations, and we can try to discover ways to stop these images in their tracks. The "triggers" that evoke these painful memories may be something like shopping in a particular store, driving down a certain stretch of roadway, dining in a particular restaurant, and so forth. After you identify these triggers, avoid them as much as possible, at least for the time-being.

Another way of overcoming painful memories is to look at the circumstances from a different perspective. This is sometimes called looking for the "silver lining in every cloud." It is a powerful way to keep our minds from dwelling too much on the pain and anguish we feel and to bring us peace in the midst of the storm.

Although negative and painful thoughts will continue to occur from time to time, you don't have to keep entertaining them. It will be difficult, but you can consciously make an effort to focus your mind on the good things in your life. Concentrate on whatever is true, honorable, right, pure, lovely, or good in your life and let your mind dwell on those things.

7. Try to Face the Reality of Your Loss as the Shock Begins to Wane

When a child dies, we, as parents, reason that such sorrow happens to other people, but it can't be happening in our lives. Shock forces us to retreat mentally until a later time, when we can get a grip on the reality of our loss.

The length of time we remain stuck in shock varies. This stage can last for an incredibly long time if we refuse to face reality and to deal with our grief. To remain in this stage for weeks or even months, most likely means that a person is suffering from unhealthy grief. So, as shock begins to wane, it is vitally important you allow yourself to face the reality of your loss and to begin to process all of the emotions you are feeling.

Wolfelt writes that "this need requires that we embrace the pain of our loss—something we naturally don't want to do. It is easier to avoid, repress, or push away the pain of grief than it is to confront it."[10] He adds that although the only way you can address your grief is by facing the pain, you will probably need to embrace your pain in small "doses," because you could not survive if you were to experience all the pain at once.

---

[10] Wolfelt, *Healing Your Grieving Heart*, p. 4.

8. Read Inspirational Materials for Solace and Emotional Release

Another way of obtaining solace or emotional release is to read works of poetry, written from either a secular or a religious perspective.

Poetry achieves its effects by rhythm, sound patterns, imagery and a loftiness of tone that not only provides comfort, but also brings, for some people, a release of emotions through crying. This can be especially helpful to bereaved parents in early grief because denial and shock sometimes prevent us from experiencing the intensity of our emotions or from shedding tears.

Chapter 2

Coping with Emotions and Loneliness

After going through the shock-and-denial stage, most people enter the second stage of grief which involves emotional suffering and loneliness. As a bereaved parent, you face the possibility, however, that you may find yourself reverting back and forth among stages or totally skipping some phases of the grief process.[1]

Don't be upset with yourself if, for example, you find yourself temporarily going back into shock even after you think you are well past this stage. There are fleeting moments when we see beyond our numbness and begin to acknowledge our loss. There are other times when reality seems too horrific, and we deny it hopelessly. After what

---

[1] Granger E. Westberg, *Good Grief Grief: A Constructive Approach to the Problem of Loss* (Minneapolis: Augsburg Fortress Press, 1979), pp. 20-21.

seems an interminable period of struggle along this pathway, you eventually will accept your child's death.

9. Allow Yourself to Process the Emotions You Are Feeling

As shock begins to wear off, you are finally able to feel the intensity of your grief and move into the second phase of grieving. The insulation of the first phase is gone and you are left feeling raw and painfully exposed. You may experience a wide range of emotions, including anger, guilt, frustration, fear, panic, and despair.

But Rando explains that "feeling and expressing your emotions is one of the most critical requirements of grief. If you do not find an acceptable way to express all your feelings of grief, you will not be able to resolve it."[2]

Right now you may not be able to identify all your feelings over the loss and its consequences. But the important thing is that you need to allow yourself to express your emotions. Your method does not necessarily matter as long as you release your feelings and do not cause harm to yourself or others.

10. Give Yourself Permission to Cry

The expression of grief is a natural part of our human experience. Yet we somehow get the idea that the tears of

---

[2]Therese A. Rando, *How to Go on Living When Someone You Love Dies* (New York: Bantam Books, 1991), p. 248.

grief are out of place in our modern world. Society implies that crying is somehow "bad" for us and tries to remove our natural and healthy expressions of sorrow by replacing them with expressions such as: "Be a man!" or "Dry up those tears!"

But it's OK to cry. James R. White, who wrote *Grief: Our Path Back to Peace*, observes that "men are often ashamed by the emotions they feel when grieving, but there is no reason for shame. [W]e dare not shortchange ourselves simply because our society has a very unrealistic view of what it means to be a 'man.'"[3]

A world without emotions would be a cold, indifferent place where there would be no appreciation of the wonder of a rainbow, the majesty of a sunrise, or the beauty of a mountain range. There would be no feelings of joy when a baby is born and no exuberance when something momentous occurred. Our lives would be bland; we would be like robots just going through the motions.

11. Remember Happy Moments

One aspect of the emotional suffering stage involves our bittersweet remembrances of the past. We recall memories of events which occurred before the loss of our child, and they often bring us to tears.

A way to combat the melancholy nature of memories is to make a positive experience out of your recollections.

---

[3] James R. White, *Grieving: Our Path Back to Peace* (Minneapolis: Bethany House Publishers, 1997), p. 50.

Go get the family photo album you've been hiding away, bring it out, open the pages, and change your negative remembrances into a positive experience as you recall the memories brought back by those old photos. Your tears will flow for sure, but why not allow some joyful tears as you dwell on uplifting thoughts about your child's accomplishments, personality, or unique human traits?

Actively remember the special qualities of the child who has died, and commemorate in your heart the life that was lived. Remember the joy of knowing them and the contributions they made during their lifetime. In this way you are not only preventing your memories from becoming disabling, you also benefit from the therapeutic value in recalling happy memories. In the process you will become empowered as you take charge of the quality of your memories rather than letting the memories take charge of you.

12. Combat Loneliness by Shopping, Running Errands, or Corresponding with Others

For bereaved parents, the feelings of isolation and loneliness associated with losing a child can be overwhelming. When you find yourself alone in your despair, you need to find ways to reduce your isolation. Westberg advises that mourners should not remain alone in their grief because "we all need the warm affection and encouragement of those about us. As we are the recipients of such affection, it makes it easier for us to sense that our present attitude of shutting out all new opportunities for meaningful living is unrealistic."[4]

For example, you can combat feelings of isolation by doing such things as going shopping or running errands. Go to the nearest mall, wander through the various stores, and visit with salespersons or strike up conversations with other shoppers as they lounge in waiting areas such as food courts. Or invent errands, like paying your local bills in person instead of mailing. Find whatever excuses you can to get yourself propelled away from the isolation of your home.

When we are unable to actually be with someone else, we can also compensate by correspondence through letters, telephone, e-mail and so forth. Sharing your feelings with friends through written words can be very therapeutic. You will be most fortunate if you can find a pen pal who shows sensitivity, responds quickly, and remains steadfast in corresponding with you through letters or email. One advantage of written correspondence is that it can be done at any time of the day or night.

Keep in mind that when you correspond with others through written or spoken words, the possibility always exists that they will say something painful or discouraging. People often make klutzy mistakes, so don't be angry, but just forgive the person and search elsewhere for a more understanding person among your friends.

---

[4]Westberg, *Good Grief*, p. 58.

13. Take Care of Your Health

When you are experiencing the pain and loneliness of the loss of your child, a danger exists that you may respond in ways that adversely impact your life, such as abusing drugs or alcohol or other chemicals. People who abuse these substances face an increased risk of becoming dependent or addicted to them, because with increased use the amount of the drug needed to dull the pain escalates and the severity of the reaction to substance withdrawal increases.

In addition to the risk of addiction and the destruction of brain cells, the use of alcohol and other drugs can delay the grieving process. You avoid accepting reality.

Of course, a more serious side effect of using drugs is an increased risk of committing suicide to avoid emotional suffering. The thought of suicide may be the desperate reaction of a parent to incredible feelings of hopelessness or despair brought on by the seeming lack of positive solutions to the dilemma of the loss of a child. Dr O'Connor emphasizes that, in cases such as this, suicide can be "a reaction to incredible stress, fear, and depression, an act of desperation. It is not a rational 'action,' but a 'reaction' to [what is perceived to be] an intolerable circumstance currently operating in the life of a person."[5]

---

[5]Nancy O'Connor, *Letting Go With Love: The Grieving Process* (Tucson, AZ: La Mariposa Press, 1984), p. 153.

Suicide has often been referred to as the ultimate cry for help. If you have been contemplating suicide or someone you love has been giving verbal or non-verbal clues about self-destruction, contact your local Suicide Prevention Service immediately. Don't wait! Suicidal emotions or behavior should always be taken very seriously.

Most cities in the United States have crisis intervention centers (names may vary in different locales) where people can call to talk to caring people trained in suicide prevention. They can talk you through the immediate crisis, refer you to competent counseling, or console a suicidal family member.

Refuse to dwell on a negative picture of your circumstances. Instead, dwell on the hopeful prospect of healing, recovery, and restoration. Although at times you may feel like giving up, don't. You can survive your child's death and lead a rich life.

Chapter 3

Coping with Depression

Following the death of a child, parents often find themselves slipping into depression. Judith R. Bernstein, author of *When the Bough Breaks: Forever After the Death of a Son or Daughter*, emphasizes the traumatic quality of the loss: "When a child dies, the very ground on which we depend for stability heaves and quakes and the rightness and orderliness of our existence are destroyed. The loss of a child is shattering, unique among losses."[1]

Although we may grieve deeply for the loss of an aged parent, relative, or friend, the predictability of the universe remains intact, for we understand the mortality of elderly persons. But when a child dies, the order of nature is thrown askew and our world is turned upside

---

[1] Judith R. Bernstein, *When the Bough Breaks: Forever After the Death of a Son or Daughter* (Kansas City: Andrews McMeal Publishing, 1998), p. 30.

down. It isn't surprising then that many bereaved mothers and fathers may suffer from depression.

14. Don't be Ashamed If You Become Depressed

Depression is an affliction that can be as mild as a "blue mood," which leaves you feeling temporarily sad, or as severe as clinical depression, which can lead to hospitalization. Mild depression is a common reaction to significant loss and a normal part of the grief process. A bereaved parent may lack energy or motivation, feel helpless, hopeless or powerless, or experience a myriad of other emotional symptoms often associated with depression. If you are feeling blue or depressed, just remember that it's a normal part of the grieving process.

But deep or clinical depression is more serious. When you reach the point where you feel incapable of coping with the demands of everyday life, clinical depression may have set in. Depression of this degree is serious and may require professional intervention. Do not wait to seek professional help.[2]

15. Share Your Thoughts with Family and Friends

One way to deal with depression is to share your feelings with family and friends. Talking to someone will

---

[2]See: Bernstein, *When the Bough Breaks*, pp. 26-31, for more information about clinical depression.

help you cope with the emotional pain and work through your grief. This may take many months of introspection, self-examination, and discussion. Holding your feelings in can contribute to depression. In addition to family and friends, a pastor or mental health professional can also make a good listener.

It should be remembered, however, that communication between bereaved fathers and mothers can be problematic at times. Sanders emphasizes that understanding the grief of a spouse is never an easy task, "because men and women have been socialized to fill different roles. A man is socialized to be unemotional, self-sufficient, and in control. A woman, on the other hand, is socialized to be nurturing and empathetic, the family communicator."[3]

Rando notes that a dad will generally focus on "controlling his feelings, when what he needs to do is to identify and express them."[4] On the other hand, mothers are prone to express their emotions and to accept help from others but have more difficulty expressing anger.

To avoid family conflict, it is important that moms and dads allow for the differences in grief style. Every person grieves differently, so it would be unwise for you to try to force a change in your partner's style. But you can give your husband or wife the permission to open up in expressions of grief if he or she so wishes. For instance, if

---

[3] Catherine M. Sanders, *How to Survive the Loss of a Child* (New York: Three Rivers Press, 1998), pp. 10-11.
[4] Therese A. Rando, *How to Go on Living When Someone You Love Dies* (New York: Bantam Books, 1991), p. 70.

you are the husband, you can let your wife know that it is all right for her to show anger, and if you are the wife, you can let your husband know it is OK for him to express his feelings verbally or through tears.

In cases where bereaved fathers and mothers are greatly out of synch with each other, support should be sought from sources other than the spouse. Comfort lies in seeking solace from neutral sources among other family and friends, leaving the spouse at peace and removing pressure from the marriage. It should be emphasized that different styles of mourning are to be expected and that there is no right or wrong way to grieve.

As you and your spouse continue to work on your grief, remember that it is important for both of you to strive to maintain hope during the process. As time goes on, the pain of grief will dissipate and life eventually will have meaning for you again. Let me assure you that these are not hopes that would invalidate your current intense grief, but realistic beliefs are needed as you respond to the death of your beloved child.

16. Eat Well, Exercise and Get Adequate Sleep

The depression resulting from the loss of a child can bring about physical reactions. Our minds and our bodies function together, so stress in one area can cause stress in another. Bereavement can affect our physical health.[5]

---

[5]Nancy O'Connor, *Letting Go With Love: The Grieving Process* (Tucson, AZ: La Mariposa Press, 1984), p. 17-21.

Some of the physical symptoms common in grief are decreased energy, decreased or increased sexual desire, dizziness, empty feelings, gastrointestinal disturbances, heart palpations, lack of appetite, lethargy, irritability, nervousness, physical exhaustion, restlessness, shortness of breath, sleep difficulties (too much or too little), tearfulness, trembling, tendency to sigh, and weight loss or gain.

During this period, increased stress can adversely affect your ability to sleep. You may have trouble falling asleep or waking up too early. Exhaustion is common. Some people lose their appetites and fail to eat healthy food. Others eat more as a reaction to stress. Because of physical exhaustion or apathy, a grief-stricken parent may also neglect physical exercise.

It is very important that you work to maintain your health through a well-balanced diet, physical exercise, and proper sleep.

Strive to eat balanced meals in proper portions. Remember also to eat even at times when you are not hungry, but not to overeat if you are prone to using food for comfort. In addition, don't forget to drink lots of water. Grief can sometimes override the thirst mechanism and lead to dehydration. Water, juices, and decaffeinated beverages are all acceptable, but alcoholic drinks should be avoided.

Exercise regularly. Jog, walk, bicycle, or do aerobics in a systematic manner. Regular exercise promotes physical health as well as mental health. It helps relieve stress, anxiety, depression, and feelings of aggression.

Outdoor exercise in the sun and fresh air can be especially uplifting emotionally.

Feelings of exhaustion and fatigue are common in grief. If you feel tired during the day, lie down for short rest periods or take an afternoon nap if you can. Your body is telling you it needs rest, so pamper yourself by getting extra daytime rest. Try to develop a relaxing bedtime routine so you're ready for sleep at night. Take your phone off the hook, shower or bathe, listen to quiet music, sip a tasteful beverage, or read a good book.

17. Embrace a Positive Coping Style

During the major life transition caused by the loss of a child, you will make choices about how you will respond. O'Connor points out that there are four possible responses to change: (1) *Conservation*, which involves attempting to remain in the present or to return to the past; (2) *Revolution*, or aggressively rejecting the past, denying the present, and damning the future; (3) *Escape*, or evading the present anguish and pain; and (4) *Transcendence,* or going beyond grief and loss to reorganize your life.[6]

Attempting to shut out the anguish of present suffering by mentally remaining in the refuge of the past is a feature of the conservation style. It is a way of living life as if nothing has changed. A parent who sets up a permanent shrine to a deceased child and who continues to live as though the child has not died is an example.

---

[6]O'Connor, *Letting Go With Love*, p. 159-161, 164.

The revolution style of coping is a way of denying the present pain by rejecting former values, beliefs, and lifestyle. For instance, a parent who decides to join a motorcycle gang and who rebels and fights against everything that formerly provided stability in life is using the revolution style.

Escape is a negative style of coping in which a parent abuses the use of alcohol, drugs or other addictive substances, or tries to escape through behaviors such as gambling and promiscuity. An individual who uses the escape method is refusing to think on the past or to analyze feelings of the present to come to terms with grief or with life.

The transcendent method is a positive coping style which utilizes honesty with self, openness to self-examination, reflection on feelings, and flexibility to change. Don't miss out on the resolution of your grief by refusing to deal with it in a positive manner.

18. Seek Out Information on the Grieving Process

It has often been said that knowledge is power. Mourning moms and dads desperately need instructions on what to expect, what is normal, and how to confront the dilemmas that face them. Many grieving parents report the experience of being pulled into a violent eddy — feeling that they are spinning out of control. Confusion compounds the situation. They feel themselves swirling in turbulent, uncharted waters without a guide or chart to tell them how to cope or mourn.

Bernstein writes that "mourners desperately need to find order and predictability. Books and groups of other bereaved parents provide an anchor. It is reassuring to see that others are indeed experiencing the same violent, chaotic emotions."[7]

Many good books on grief and mourning can be found at local and school libraries and bookstores. Bereaved parents who want to search for additional assistance in dealing with grief can also find additional help at their library in the form of internet resources on the subject. Capable librarians are available to give assistance in the search.

For many parents, participation in a support group, which serves as a frame of reference by providing models, ideas, and suggestions about how others have dealt with grief, can be most helpful. By joining a self-help support group, you will come into contact with a group of parents going through experiences similar to yours. Members give support to one another as they share information, provide encouragement, and give practical advice for managing grief. As you listen to their stories, take comfort in knowing that you are not alone in your grief. Bereaved Parents of the USA and Compassionate Friends are two examples of excellent support groups.

The Internet has numerous informative resources for mourners, including articles about grief, Internet chat

---

[7]Bernstein, *When the Bough Breaks*, pp. 5-6.

groups set up for bereaved parents, and sites devoted to organizations that help grievers. Here are some suggestions:

- Compassionate Friends (international) at www.compassionatefriends.org;
- The Bereaved Parents of the USA at www.bereavedparentsusa.org;
- The Candlelighters Childhood Cancer Foundation, www.candlelighters.org;
- Mothers Against Drunk Driving (MADD) at www.madd.org;
- Parents of Murdered Children at www.pomc.com;
- Sudden Infant Death Syndrome Support at www.EarlyAngels.com;
- Pregnancy and Infant Loss Support at www.nationalshareoffice.com.

19. Obtain Professional Help If You Need It

Emotions can control our lives if we fail to make progress in the work of processing our grief. The death of a child ranks as the most significant death loss that anyone can ever experience. Sanders reports that a child's death "takes much longer to process, because the factors involved are compounded."[8] She notes that some of the compounding factors faced by parents are: resolving guilt and anger; relinquishing the parent-child bond; and

---

[8]Catherine M. Sanders, *How to Survive the Loss of a Child* (New York: Three Rivers Press, 1998), p. viii.

grieving not only for the loss of their child, but also for lost aspects of themselves.

The grief after the loss of a child is one of the hardest and longest types of loss to face, yet we know that it is in experiencing our grief and in coming to terms with our own feelings that we can actively move through grief toward healing and restoration. As you endeavor to work through your grief, it is important for you to monitor your emotions to see if you are making progress and to seek professional help if needed.

Sanders points out that there are some general indicators that can signal when a parent probably needs additional help in dealing with bereavement.[9] They include (1) avoiding friends and relatives rather than honestly communicating with them; (2) failing to eat properly, get enough sleep or tend to basic self-care needs; (3) denying your loss; (4) having obsessive self-destructive or suicidal thoughts; (5) taking your anger out on people close to you or on yourself; (6) becoming immobilized by grief and unable to see hope for the future; (7) masking your feelings through self-medication, alcohol, or other substance abuse; (8) engaging in foolish acts, such as becoming addicted to gambling or other compulsive behaviors; (9) having a history of severe emotional problems; (10) having a feeling that you are falling apart or are no longer in control; (11) having a lack of interest or joy in life even though sufficient time has passed; (12) being consistently told by family or friends that they think

---

[9]Sanders, *How to Survive the Loss of a Child*.

you need professional assistance; (13) having your minister or your personal physician refer you to a mental health professional.

Once you decide you are interested in obtaining professional assistance, you will need to find a qualified mental health clinician who fits with you. You can obtain referrals from sources such as friends or relatives; mental health organizations, members of the clergy, your personal physician, support group lists of preferred experts, and so forth. As you look for a therapist, rid yourself of the notion that depression is something to be ashamed of. Treat it as you would any physical illness that invades your life and requires treatment for renewed health.

In your search for a qualified expert, it is important that you find someone who not only has professional training in the mental health field, but who also has experience in understanding bereavement following the loss of a child. In addition, you should find someone you are personally comfortable with and who you think is helping you to comprehend and process your grief. Look around until you can find someone with whom you can really connect. At the same time, bear in mind that counseling and therapy take time because the resolution of grief is difficult and slow work.

Chapter 4

Coping with Panic

After the death of your child, you may find that you are unable to get your mind off your loss or focus on routine matters. This may cause anxiety and a feeling that you are losing control.

Keep in mind, however, that grief is not just sadness, but a whole host of emotions. This includes difficulty making conversation, disorganized behavior, flashbacks, hyperactivity, inability to make decisions, irritability, loss of interest in personal appearance, preoccupation with events surrounding the death, repetitive dreams, and a sense of meaninglessness. These and other symptoms can rapidly alternate or recur, which in turn can foster a feeling of panic.[1]

---

[1] Therese A. Rando, *How to Go on Living When Someone You Love Dies* (New York: Bantam Books, 1991), pp. 25-37.

In addition, you may be plagued by questions like: *How can I bear this horrible tragedy? How will I survive? What am I supposed to do to be a "good griever"?*

You will need to understand that these problems and questions are only temporary conditions that will pass with time. Don't panic. You are simply experiencing a normal part of grief. Other bereaved parents have traveled this same pathway and survived. You will too.

20. Don't Panic If You Are Unable to Get Your Loss off Your Mind

As a grieving parent, you may find yourself becoming concerned because you can think of nothing but your loss. You try very hard to get your mind off the subject, but you can't. This single-minded focus on your grief seems to be affecting your personal relationships and job performance.

For a bereaved parent, interaction in close personal relationships can be hampered because the distraction of grief causes you to be less adept in communicating with others. For example, when people talk to you or ask you questions, you may have to ask them over and over to repeat what was said. Your effectiveness on your job can be affected, too, because you may have problems concentrating, processing information, organizing facts, or making decisions relevant to your work.[2]

---

[2]Granger E. Westberg, *Good Grief: A Constructive Approach to the Problem of Loss* (Minneapolis: Augsburg Fortress Press, 1979), p. 43.

Socially, your lack of interest in former values may lead you to want to spend less time with those who place great value on climbing the social ladder or acquiring creature comforts. Because your focus on "things" has diminished, you find materialistic values unacceptable. In addition, you feel a sense of impatience with people who complain about trivial matters, discuss inconsequential subjects, or engage in petty gossip.[3]

It is important for you to realize that preoccupation with grief is a reflection of the internal grief work being done as you sift through every aspect of the death. This single-mindedness excludes other concerns, for you are deeply preoccupied with the internal reality of the severed relationship, with your understanding of it, and with managing your reaction. This is basically why nothing else matters as much to you at this time.

An essential component of the grief process for mourning parents is the search for the cause and meaning of their child's death. In this regard, bereaved moms and dads can expect to deal with death-related questions for a long time, such as: *How did it happen? Why did it happen? How could it have been prevented? What occurred just before the death?* Our minds grow weary as we ask these questions over and over.

Yet we feel a need to understand or comprehend as best we can by piecing together a "story" that will give us

---

[3] Judith R. Bernstein, *When the Bough Breaks: Forever After the Death of a Son or Daughter* (Kansas City: Andrews McMeal Publishing, 1998), pp. 80-81.

some answers to our questions. Brook Noel writes that "we need to fact-find and uncover a beginning, middle, and end [to our story] so that we can quit the relentless questioning that keeps us from moving forward."[4] She adds that it is important for us to find answers so that we won't spend more time than necessary recycling the past and can begin to deal with the present and future.

Although some questions about a child's death can be answered, other questions regarding why it happened or how it fits into the scheme of life can be difficult to answer. For example, a parent whose child commits suicide may never know why the child chose to end his or her own life. It is unwise for such a parent to torture him or herself with questions on a subject for which there may be incomplete or unknown answers. Rather, the parent may need to just "let it go" and move on.

21. Don't Worry if You Are Unable to Focus on Simple Tasks

As a grieving parent, you may be wondering why you are having difficulty focusing on even simple tasks. Although concentration is difficult after most losses, when a child dies, parents may find it impossible to focus on routine matters. A jumble of thoughts continually bombards our minds as we struggle desperately to absorb

---

[4] Brook Noel, *Grief Steps: 10 Steps to Regroup, Rebuild, and Renew After Any Life Loss* (Fredonia, WI: Champion Press, LTD., 2004), pp. 108-109.

the shock of the horrible tragedy that has befallen us. Even usual distractions, like watching television or light reading, no longer offer an escape, because our minds simply cannot quit racing long enough to allow us to focus.

In fact, as Sanders observes, even "our habitual tasks now require forethought. Before the death, there were things we usually did without thinking about them, like making the bed, straightening the kitchen, or cooking. But after such a loss, simply preparing breakfast can be an impossible task."[5] Until parents have had the chance to integrate the loss of a child into their lives, they usually experience a long period of confusion and loss of concentration. As they try to get a handle on their chaotic emotions, they experience a continuing inability to readily focus on daily activities that need to be done.

Your grief may also cause you to be highly distracted, disoriented, and befuddled. For instance, on occasion you may find yourself arriving at a destination and not recalling how you got there, stopping at green lights rather than red, or receiving a traffic ticket because you were speeding but didn't realize you were. Situations such as this can be dangerous, both to you and to others, so diligence should be exercised. Letting someone else drive or taking public transportation is a safer alternative for you at this time.

In addition, grief will cause you to have problems in thinking through decisions or making choices. For this

---

[5]Catherine M. Sanders, *Surviving Grief and Learning to Live Again* (New York: John Wiley and Sons, Inc., 1992), pp. 126.

reason, it is advisable for you to refrain from making major decisions relating to such things as job, housing, or relationship changes soon after your loss. You may have to temporarily rely on other trusted sources of support for objective feedback on problems and decisions. In minor areas where memory lapses or lack of concentration cause problems, you can give yourself support by using lists and agendas to keep your thinking clear.

22. Be Patient with Yourself as You Go Through the Grief Process

As time goes on and the severity of your grief does not seem to dissipate as quickly as you wish, you may begin to panic that you will never "get over" your grief. It is important to remember that you can't chart out a course or determine a time frame for grief.[6] The fact is that in a sense you will never actually "get over it." The relationship that was yours with your son or daughter will never be there again in this life. So, in some ways you will always be "in the process."

People often quote the maxim that time heals all wounds, meaning that if we just wait long enough, the pain of grief will go away. The pain never goes away completely, but it will lessen. The therapeutic aspect of time is that it can allow you to put things in perspective, process feelings, adapt to change, and attend to your grief

---

[6]Alan D. Wolfelt, *Healing Your Grieving Heart: 100 Practical Ideas* (Fort Collins, CO: Companion Press, 1998), p. 57.

work. These experiences, plus the passage of time, reduce your pain. But the passage of time can only help you to successfully adapt to your loss if you are actively engaged in your grief work.

Many people also incorrectly assume that as grief diminishes with time, it goes from high to low in a straight line, and that once it declines it never erupts again. Actually, the intensity of your grief will fluctuate over time and have many ups and downs. Some of these fluctuations are caused by events such as anniversaries, holidays, and changes in factors relating to you grief, such as diminishing social support or the presence of other stresses in your life. When this happens, you may find it quite frustrating to feel your grief anew after experiencing a break from it.

Grief takes much time and energy and will progress at an uneven pace. Some segments of your mourning may be done at one period and other aspects may be stored away to be dealt with later. You will alternate between making progress and backsliding, but you will never go as far back as you were in the beginning. Be patient and do not place unrealistic expectations on yourself or other family members in regard to a time frame for healing.

23. Don't Allow Others to Push You Through Grief According to Their Time Frames

Some friends may expect you to return to your "old self" or to "get better" before you have had time to grieve. Bernstein points out that many times they think there is a schedule to follow in grief: "Self-appointed experts, professionals, clergy, and well-meaning friends and family are ready with solace, exhortations, and ultimately the admonition that it's time to 'get on with your life,' as if life could ever be the same."[7]

When you're in the throes of grief, it's easy to feel like you're doing it all wrong, like you're reacting abnormally. Friends and professionals can compound the uncertainty when they suggest you should be conducting your grief according to their time frame. Don't allow friends, or anyone else, to push you through the mourning process or to set a time frame for you. Recognize that your grief will be unique to you and to your particular loss. It will be shaped by your own personal characteristics and by the unique group of factors that describe your particular loss.

Remember, too, that it doesn't make any difference what others think. It's your loss and your grief. We each have to grieve at our own pace, even if that pace is different from what our friends would expect or like. It is true however, that the course of mourning can proceed more quickly for some than for others. Some grieving parents find purpose and meaning quite quickly, while other parents remain in the deepest shadows much longer. Most of the time, however, the journey through grief is difficult work and takes a lot of time, determination, and persistent effort.

---

[7] Judith R. Bernstein, *When the Bough Breaks: Forever After the Death of a Son or Daughter* (Kansas City: Andrews McMeal Publishing, 1998), p. 6.

Chapter 5

Coping with Guilt

The "natural" order of life, we are taught, is that children die after their parents, not before them. When a child goes first, it is not unusual for parents to feel overwhelmed by a sense of guilt and regret.

24. Don't Assume Responsibility for Things You Cannot Control

Keep in mind that as a parent, you are experiencing one of the most dreaded events that can occur in life, so it is normal for you to feel tremendous guilt. Guilt is a natural by-product of grief no matter what the loss, but the guilt of a parent is doubly pronounced. When something happens to our children, we immediately blame ourselves because we feel responsible for them. We reason that if we had been more on guard, the death would never have occurred.

We live in a society that expects parents to be totally responsible for their children's care. If something happens to our child, we feel, as parents, that we are at fault, that we should have been taking better care to prevent such harm. "If only" are two words uttered over and over again as we blame ourselves for what happened to our child. Instead of moving forward, we scroll backward to recall the "if onlys" of a past we cannot change or recover. As we continue the self-blame game, we halt the grieving process. Guilt is completely unproductive and will only delay your recovery and healing.[1]

You may be in the process of searching your soul to discover what it is that you did or did not do that could have prevented your child's death. These thoughts and feelings are common, but know that in time they will pass. In the meantime, focus on being compassionate toward yourself.

25. Make a Distinction Between Real and Unjustified Guilt

There are basically two types of guilt in grief. Guilt that is out of proportion to the event is called unjustified or illegitimate guilt. On the other hand, when there is a direct cause-and-effect relationship between something

---

[1] Nancy O'Connor, *Letting Go With Love: The Grieving Process* (Tucson, AZ: La Mariposa Press, 1984), p. 138-140.

you did or failed to do that caused harm to the deceased, that type of guilt is considered real or legitimate guilt.[2]

Unjustified guilt is the normal consequence of the parent/child relationship that is, by its nature, flawed. Keep in mind that parents are human beings and, as such, make mistakes and have ambivalent feelings in relationships. Unjustified guilt often comes from overly high standards you may have placed upon yourself.

For example, after your child's death, you may have said something like: "I should have been able to prevent my child's death." Or, "During our relationship, I never should have felt anger toward my youngster." Comments such as these reveal that you have been holding unrealistic expectations for yourself. In many cases, even if you have been an exemplary parent and have handled everything in the best possible way, you will nevertheless focus on something you think you did wrong or did not do at all.

To determine if you are experiencing unjustified guilt, you may want to discuss your feelings with a trusted and nonjudgmental person, either professional or nonprofessional, who can help you examine events rationally to decide if you did act in the best way possible under the circumstance. If you are indeed experiencing false guilt, don't continue to harbor guilt or regret that you didn't do or say more.

---

[2]Therese A. Rando, *How to Go on Living When Someone You Love Dies* (New York: Bantam Books, 1991), pp. 34-35.

Who can find a time when we were perfect. When our child dies, there is always something more we could have done; there is always something more we could have said; there is always something more. Cast aside unjustified guilt or regrets, both those thrust upon you and those of your own making.

Legitimate or real guilt occurs when your guilt is appropriate to the situation, when there is a direct cause-and-effect role between something you did or did not do and harm which resulted to your deceased child. This may have been a purposeful action or inaction which caused harm. Or, it may have been an unintentional action or lack of action that produced hurt to your child.

An example of a purposeful act is the highly publicized case in which a suicidal mother intentionally drove a car, with her little children inside, into a lake. The mom changed her mind about suicide and saved herself by jumping out of the car, but left her small children inside to drown.

An instance of an unintentional act might occur when parents in charge of watching out for a child fail to perform that responsibility through inattention or oversight. An example of inattention could be the case of a parent who doses off poolside while supervising a child, resulting in the drowning death of the youngster. An example of oversight might be when a mother and father both presume the other is supervising a child, but each fails to communicate the fact to the other parent, and, as a consequence, the child dies. A case in point would be a child left sleeping in a car in hot weather, because each parent thought the other had taken the child from the vehicle.

In cases where failure of a parent to protect a child is not purposeful, the father or mother responsible will nevertheless probably suffer from a tremendous sense of guilt and blame. If you are a parent who is experiencing real guilt because of an unintentional act or inaction, you may need to seek professional psychiatric assistance in order to deal with your sense of guilt. It is vitally important that you come to terms with the fact that what happened was an accident so you can forgive yourself.

26. Don't Blame Yourself for Your Child's Suicide

For parents, the suicide of a child is one of the most difficult deaths with which to cope. Such a death burdens the mourning parent with extra guilt and prolongs the healing process. Intense guilt is quite common because when a child commits suicide parents tend to think they could have prevented it. Parental self-reproach is also prominent because fathers and mothers often blame themselves for not recognizing the depth of their child's despair and for not taking action. Typically they ask themselves over and over how they failed as parents.[3]

If your child has completed suicide, no doubt you will mentally pore over and over the events of the days and weeks preceding the death searching for answers and

---

[3]Catherine M. Sanders, *Surviving Grief and Learning to Live Again* (New York: John Wiley and Sons, Inc., 1992), pp. 113-115.

trying to make sense of this senseless event. You will also ask questions that can never be answered because the only person who can verify the answers is dead. You will ask, "Why did my child do this?" "Why didn't my youngster tell me things were so bad?" "Why couldn't I stop my offspring from doing this?" "What did I do wrong?"

These and numerous other questions will consume you if you let them. You can spend years going over detail after detail preceding the event and punish yourself needlessly for what you think you should have said or done that might have made a difference. But actually, guilt of this nature accomplishes nothing except to make you feel worse and prolong your emotional misery.

Don't let guilt hold you hostage. Suicidal death can have incredible power over the lives of surviving parents and other family members, leaving them with confusion and guilt over the death. Whatever happened in the past, keep in mind that you did the best you could at the time. Now you need to forgive yourself so you can begin to move on with the rest of your life. Don't allow past memories to retain the power to ruin your present life.

What follows are some suggestions for parents who have lost a child to suicide: focus on what you were able to do for your child, not on what you didn't do; talk to friends or family; seek out support groups for survivors of suicide; talk to a professional counselor trained in working with families of suicides; learn to forgive yourself and move on with your life.

27. Talk to a Professional About Your Feelings of Guilt

Following the death of a child, bereaved parents often struggle with a host of guilt feelings. For instance, if a youngster died from disease or illness, surviving parents may have lingering doubts about decisions made regarding treatment, such as whether they might have missed early symptoms, whether they allowed the child to go through too much treatment, and so forth. Past decisions in regard to care of the child are questioned endlessly even though parents may have actually done the very best that they could in caring for their child.

Mourning fathers and mothers may also feel guilt concerning our helplessness and inability to save our children. No matter what we did, we were unable to make things better. Consequently, we feel inadequate and guilty that we could not prevent the death. Survivor guilt may occur too. The meaning of life is questioned, because we wonder why we should be allowed to go on living, when our child has been deprived of a future here on earth.

Guilt about ambivalent feelings is likewise common. It is perfectly normal that conflicting feelings should exist, yet we feel guilty that while our child was still alive we may have experienced anger or resentment directed toward the young person. No relationship is perfect. All relationships are mixtures of positive and negative emotions. Yet, following our youngster's death, we may dwell on memories of negative emotions until they become gigantic in our minds, and we may torture ourselves with built for having conflicting feelings toward a son or daughter.

Another source of guilt is perceived misdeeds. A parent may have failed in some aspect of life, and now he or she sees the child's death as punishment for mistakes or misdeeds. For instance, an alcoholic parent may interpret the loss of a child as punishment for the parent's excessive drinking. In addition, moms or dads may experience guilt about public reactions to the death. Despite the fact that we are fighting a heroic battle just to survive our pain, we perceive that perhaps we have failed to act in a way that society expects of us. We may think we over-reacted or under-reacted at the funeral, so we feel guilty for not acting the "right" way. What we fail to remember is that there really is no right or wrong way to grieve.

The most common types of guilt bereaved parents suffer have been examined here, but there are many other forms. It will be helpful to the progress of your grief-work if you talk about whatever kind of guilt reactions you are experiencing with someone you trust. Sanders elaborates that guilt held inside becomes destructive, but the "way to exorcize guilt is to share guilty feelings with supportive, caring people."[4]

Talk about your guilt feelings with someone you trust, or if you feel ready for group situations, seek out self-help groups. Chances are, others have experienced the same

---

[4]Sanders, *Surviving Grief and Learning to Live Again*, need page number here, p. 56.

feelings, too. In addition, don't be afraid or embarrassed to talk about your feelings of guilt with a professional qualified to counsel on the subject of parental grief. An expert counselor can give you valuable insight and advice on how to conquer your feelings of guilt.

In order to let go of guilt, you will need to constantly remind yourself that under the circumstances you did the best you could. Refuse to dwell on negative feelings of guilt.

Chapter 6

Coping with Anger

Anger is another emotion to be expected to some degree after the death of a child. The anger need not be overly intense or necessarily be displayed through screaming infuriation, but it may be seen in milder variations such as irritability, intolerance, frustration, or annoyance. The resentment we feel is a consequence of our being deprived of something greatly valued by us, our child.[1]

Feelings of anger are normal for grieving parents, although we may endeavor to sublimate these feelings. If feelings of anger do exist, it would be extremely harmful to us if we could not admit to ourselves that we are indeed irate about one or more aspects of our loss and take actions to dispel that anger.

---

[1] Therese A. Rando, *How to Go on Living When Someone You Love Dies* (New York: Bantam Books, 1991), p. 29.

28. Let Friends and Professionals Help You Cope with Your Anger

Anger in the bereaved parent comes from many things. There is anger about being deprived of a future with our child and anger about our feelings of frustration and helplessness. Anger can even be directed at society in general, at the world at large, at organized religion or a "higher being," or at any other source.

You have a right to feel your emotions. Anger is a part of your grief, a real and normal reaction to your feelings of loss, deprivation, confusion, and despair. Keep in mind, however, that resentment carried for too long can be destructive. Harry and Cheryl Salem point out that "anger is an honest emotion. We may feel angry for a few days, weeks, or even months, but, eventually, those feelings must be dealt with. Unchecked anger doesn't fix anything. It doesn't do anyone any good, and it only brings harm to the person who is angry."[2]

It is important that you quickly deal with your anger by talking with a trusted friend who can accept your rage and listen as you recount your bitter feelings. Don't hide or be ashamed of your feelings. Hiding your anger won't make it go away. You'll work it out of your system more quickly if you can bring it out into the open.

---

[2]Harry Salem and Cheryl Salem, *From Grief to Glory: Rediscovering Life After Loss* (New Kensington, PA: Whitaker House, 2003), p. 95.

29. Don't Blame Innocent Others for Your Loss

Anger may be turned inward and be experienced as depression, or it may be projected outward onto other people.[3] When we project anger onto others, often we do so because we need someone to blame for what has happened to our child. Often feelings of anger and hostility are directed toward those who are closest to us, our family members. Parents are especially prone to blame each other for the loss of a child. At times, parental anger is displaced onto other individuals, such as ambulance drivers, hospital workers, and so forth.

Of course, justified anger can stem from cases of homicide, suicide, or self-destructive behavior. For instance, if your child has been murdered, one would expect you to be enraged that someone would kill your beloved child. If your child took his or her own life, you also would be expected to be angry at the child for ending a young life and imposing tremendous heartache upon you. Anger such as this is not easily addressed or resolved.

To confront your anger, you will need to identify your feelings, admit your anger to yourself, and then communicate it to someone you trust.[4] A good friend, a professional counselor, or a pastor can help you to address your feelings of anger or rage. Another way to deal with

---

[3] See Catherine M. Sanders, *How to Survive the Loss of a Child* (New York: Three Rivers Press, 1998), p. 58, for more information about displaced anger.

[4] Nancy O'Connor, *Letting Go With Love: The Grieving Process* (Tucson, AZ: La Mariposa Press, 1984), pp. 34-35.

pent-up emotions is to release them through physical activity such as walking, running, swimming, or working out. While physical activity is helpful, it is only a temporary solution to let off steam. It will be wise for you to enroll in a longer-term program, such as counseling or group support, to assist you in getting in touch with your anger and resolving it.

30. Let a Child Who Commits Suicide Accept Responsibility for His or Her Actions

When a child dies by suicide, it is logical for the parents to feel some anger toward the youngster. Drug abuse or other self-destructive actions resulting in a child's death might also contribute to angry feelings directed toward the child. When a child commits suicide or dies as a result of risky behavior, as Sanders points out, the parents "are usually, and quite naturally, angry at the deceased child."[5]

There can be anger that the child purposely chose to leave you, anger that the child's death has thrown your life into turmoil, anger that you have been deprived of the child's companionship, and anger that the suicide deprived the child of a future. It is very sad for you to realize that you will never get to see a son or daughter grow to adulthood, possibly marry and bear children, all because of a willful act of self-destruction.

---

[5]Catherine M. Sanders, *How to Survive the Loss of a Child* (New York: Three Rivers Press, 1998), p. 59.

Recognize that you are particularly victimized by a death resulting from either suicide or self-destructive behavior and susceptible to intensified bereavement reactions. Your anger may be directed toward your deceased child, toward yourself, or toward other people. If your anger is directed toward your child, you may be uncomfortable with your anger at the one now dead. Realize, however, that your anger is normal and that you will need to confront it, not deny it.

If you are angry toward yourself, you may be assuming that you could have done something to prevent the death. For example, in regard to a suicidal death, do not place unrealistic blame or anger on yourself for missing or not responding to possible hints or clues about an impending act that now make sense to you in the light of hindsight. You will need to recognize the limits of your ability to have prevented a suicide, for none of us is ultimately responsible for or in control of another person's choices, even if that person is a child.

The same advice goes if you are angry toward another individual who failed to prevent a child's self-destructive act. For instance, you might feel anger toward someone to whom your child confided suicidal thoughts, because the person did not take proper action to prevent the death. Again, remember that hindsight is 20/20. The suicidal intentions of a child may not be recognized or taken seriously at the time by another person.

Consignment for the actions of your youngster cannot be assumed by you or by anyone else. In the final analysis, we are accountable only for our own choices, whether good or bad. Don't accept responsibility yourself or place fault on others for the purposeful self-destructive actions of your child.

31. Forgive Others and Yourself

Forgiveness can be one of the most difficult aspects to achieve in the process of working through grief. Sometimes we are unable to move forward because we need to first release our angry emotions before we can get to the place where we can actually forgive. To achieve a forgiving spirit, you must face the reality of what took place when your child died and why you are angry at someone, whether that person is ourselves, another person, our even our deceased child. Then you must process your angry emotions by choosing to give up resentments and by releasing the energy that has kept you in bondage.

But what exactly is forgiveness? Noel provides an excellent definition: "Forgiveness simply means that we acknowledge the deep pain we feel, but choose to move past that pain. We forgive those who contributed to our pain and let their actions become part of our past."[6] She adds that forgiveness doesn't mean we are condoning hurtful actions or forgetting how much we hurt. Rather,

---

[6] Brook Noel, *Grief Steps: 10 Steps to Regroup, Rebuild, and Renew After Any Life Loss* (Fredonia, WI: Champion Press, LTD., 2004), p. 129.

we are able to forgive someone despite the fact that we dislike what he or she has done.

Remember that if your anger is directed toward your deceased child because the young person took his or her own life by carelessness or by design, you must find a way to release the anger you are feeling. Or, if there was a traumatic relationship between you two while he or she was still alive, you must let go of that, too. When we lose a loved one during a rocky point in our relationship, such as during the rebellious teen years, we may recall hurtful words that were exchanged. While conflicts cannot be resolved directly with the child anymore, we can still resolve them in our hearts by letting go of anger and by practicing forgiveness.

Even when we are able to forgive others, however, we often find it difficult to forgive ourselves because we may hold ourselves to an unrealistic standard we wouldn't expect from someone else. By amplifying our own mistakes, and by holding ourselves hostage to our own perceived misdeeds, we neglect to forgive ourselves and thereby prevent forward progress in our lives.

One of the most important lessons we can learn from grief is that we don't have to suffer long years of pain because of unresolved anger toward others or even toward ourselves. We can release resentful feelings by replacing the negative feelings and bitterness at the root of our anger with the positive feelings of joy, peace, and contentment.

Chapter 7

Coping with Physical Aspects of Grief

As already mentioned, grief not only affects you emotionally, it can also affect your physical health. Doctors have connected enduring stress to a breakdown of the immune system, which consequently invites infectious diseases. According to Sanders, the ongoing stress of grief can cause changes in "blood pressure, heart rate, and the chemical makeup of blood. Prolonged grief can actually suppress our immune system, leaving us exposed to a variety of illnesses, infections, and maladies."[1]

---

[1]Catherine M. Sanders, *Surviving Grief and Learning to Live Again* (New York: John Wiley and Sons, Inc., 1992), pp. 80-81.

32. Control Your Stress

Stress overload is caused by the tremendous trauma and prolonged stress we endure in bereavement.[2] Grief uses an enormous expenditure of mental energy, which results in debilitating stress. For parents in mourning, the struggle just to survive each day can sap their strength and leave them vulnerable to illnesses such as viruses, sinusitis, or the flu. In addition, major illnesses can result, especially sicknesses that are stress-related, such as digestive tract disorders like ulcers, gastritis, or colitis. Blood pressure also may increase significantly during this period, leading to strokes or heart disease.

The continued stress of grief can keep our bodies from returning to a normal state of balance and health. Resources we normally use to cope with disease may thus be depleted, resulting in possible illness. This is why it is important for you to realize that grief can escalate into a serious health risk. You must endeavor to take care of yourself and monitor your health.

33. Don't Push Yourself Beyond the Limits of Your Physical Endurance

In an endeavor to cope with the loss of a child, some parents immerse themselves in a flurry of outside

---

[2]Nancy O'Connor, *Letting Go With Love: The Grieving Process* (Tucson, AZ: La Mariposa Press, 1984), p. 166.

activities, or in work or other pursuits.[3] Often there can be a "driven" quality to this busy activity, an obsession with throwing themselves into some pursuit so they won't have time to think about or feel their pain. They may push themselves for 16 to 18 hours a day in non-stop activities that lead to mistreatment of their bodies.

Staying busy is a way to avoid the mourning process by keeping your mind occupied on other information in an attempt to prevent contemplation on your real emotional state. Your involvement in external events is also an attempt to make the internal suffering disappear, a coping mechanism which, unfortunately, doesn't work.

The process of readjustment in the grieving process is a progressive series of measures or changes that get you from one place to another psychologically. Because grieving is a process, you will progress naturally if you just go forward in your grief work. On the other hand, if you resist the mourning process, you are in danger of breaking down physically, mentally, or both. If you have been distracting yourself from grief, realize that you will need to slow down to give yourself the chance to complete your grief work.

34. Process Your Grief

Parental grief over the loss of a child not only causes extreme sadness and hurt, it can also load us down with

---

[3]Sanders, *Surviving Grief and Learning to Live Again*, pp. 102-103.

a host of conflicting emotions, such as anger, guilt, and fear. You have a choice in regard to how you will handle your feelings and emotions. One choice is to allow yourself to feel your pain, to process your emotions, and to eventually heal. The other choice is to avoid your grief, to repress your feelings, and to postpone healing.

Grieving is the normal response to the pain and anguish of loss, but if it is repressed, denied, or internalized, it can lead to serious diseases of the body or distress of the emotions.[4] Guilty, hurtful, or angry feelings that we try to repress stay with us for years. By denying them, we merely delay and stretch out the bereavement process. It takes a lot of energy to feel emotions like guilt, rage, or frustration, but it takes more energy in the long run to hold back these emotions.

Repressing grief may actually result in psychosomatic illness, sickness resulting from the interaction between mind and body. There can be a strong correlation between illness and the way in which a great loss is handled. Physical symptoms like headaches, backaches, and other forms of physical distress can be caused by unresolved feelings of guilt, anger, and so forth that are intertwined with the grief.

In cases where repressed grief is a causal factor in illness, more than just the physical symptoms must be addressed. By obtaining psychological as well as medical assistance, a parent can understand the cause of symptoms and eradicate the illness. For psychosomatic

---

[4]O'Connor, *Letting Go With Love*, pp. 135, 170-179.

illness, healing is accomplished by grief work. By experiencing, expressing, and managing the emotions you feel, you will recover. It may take many months of self examination and professional treatment, but healing will result as you come to emotional terms with your loss.

In coping with the death of your child, you face one of the most agonizing challenges of life. Working through your grief takes energy, time, and perseverance, and you may feel like giving up at times. You have the opportunity, however, once you have processed your grief, to emerge as a stronger, more competent, and more loving person.

35. Maintain a Healthy Lifestyle During the Grief Process

To endure the difficult bereavement process and to avoid physical complications, it is essential for you to maintain a healthy lifestyle. Your physical health must be cared for not only to reduce the potential for the development of serious physical problems, but also to preserve your energy for grief work and for the important task of caring for your family.

Your health can be adversely affected if you neglect to have dental and physical check-ups when needed. Excessive tobacco use or high caffeine consumption can add to your problems, too, by making you jittery, keeping you keyed-up, and suppressing your appetite. And, of course, the negative effects alcohol or drug abuse can have on your physical health are well recognized.

Because of their deep involvement in grief, however, some bereaved parents neglect their own health. Caught up in the raw wounds of their heart and the brokenness of their spirit, they refuse to even bother to think about anything else. Keep in mind though, that as Cheryl Salem points out, "if we don't look after our own health, we will be no good to anyone else. I have found that I am a better wife, mother, and minister when I do what I need to do to keep my physical body in good working order. The same will be true for you no matter what you're facing in life."[5]

Your loved ones really need you, so take good care of yourself. Remember too that you will need to stay healthy in order to complete the difficult mourning process. There is more for you to do in life, and you must survive to be able to do it. Bear in mind that adequate care of your health will benefit your ability to cope with your loss, to meet the demands of your everyday life, and to overcome possible physical illness generated by the stress of your bereavement.

36. Give Faith a Chance to Help You Heal

Some research shows that people with strong religious convictions are better able to recover from illness and enjoy greater overall health. For example, Harold G. Koenig, M.D., a Duke University researcher who has

---

[5]Harry Salem and Cheryl Salem, *From Grief to Glory: Rediscovering Life After Loss* (New Kensington, PA: Whitaker House, 2003), p. 64.

spent many years studying the link between religion and health and is the author of *The Handbook of Religion and Health*, writes that "there is good science-based research showing an association between religion and good health. These are prospective studies with large samples showing that religion is related to lower blood pressure, greater longevity, and certainly better mental health."[6]

---

[6]This quote is taken from a Web MD archive feature, "Is Religion Good Medicine?" by Salynn Boyles (March 13, 2002), which discusses both sides of the debate over whether there is sufficient scientific research linking religion and health.

Chapter 8

Coping with Life Changes

After the loss of a son or daughter, mourning parents notice changes in almost every aspect of their lives, including ways in which they relate to their spouses, to their surviving children, and to their friends.

They also often experience changes within themselves in terms of personal beliefs about life and death, values, priorities and faith. In addition, they can notice changes associated with key life events, such as holidays, birthdays, and anniversaries.

37. Strive to Maintain a Good Relationship with Your Spouse

After a child's death, spouses should be supportive, caring, and loving toward one another. But it doesn't always happen that way. Sometimes spouses drift apart. Instead of grieving together, they become privately immersed in their own mourning.

Of course, no one expects them to grieve in the same way. One may want to discuss the pain, while the other does not; one may find comfort in work, while the other feels overwhelmed; one may want to remove memory-triggering articles and photographs from the home, while the other wants them to remain; one may want to protect surviving children from their grief, while the other tries to remain open; one may want to resume sex, while the other is uninterested; one may find comfort in religion, while the other isn't consoled; or one may have trouble releasing feelings and requesting support, while the other has difficulty expressing anger.[1]

Because of these and numerous other differences in parental grieving, it isn't surprising that studies have shown that marital discord and divorce are common after a child's death. It has been estimated that between 75 to 90 percent of all married couples have serious problems after the loss of a son or daughter.[2] It is vitally important, therefore, that you strive to maintain a good relationship with your spouse. A nonjudgmental attitude is necessary, along with a sustained effort to just be there for each other. Don't worry about trying to communicate verbally or trying to do the "right thing." Easy ways to be

---

[1] Therese A. Rando, *How to Go on Living When Someone You Love Dies* (New York: Bantam Books, 1991), pp. 171-173.

[2] Catherine M. Sanders, *How to Survive the Loss of a Child* (New York: Three Rivers Press, 1998), pp. viii, 10.

supportive and to nurture one another are the simple acts of touching, hugging, and showing signs of kindness and affection.

38. Help Your Surviving Children Cope with the Loss of Their Sibling

Surviving children in a family will greatly suffer from the loss of a sibling. When a child dies, the remaining children can have a difficult time in discharging their grief.[3] They may, like parents, (1) experience survival guilt, or (2) they may feel their parents are abandoning them emotionally, or (3) they may feel life has lost its innocence or luster. Let's examine each of these conditions.

First of all, siblings, like parents, sometimes feel that they should have been the ones to die — that they are less needed by society than the lost child. Children may also feel responsible for the death, recalling angry emotions they felt toward the child before he or she died and remembering times they said childish things like "I wish you were dead." Then, when the brother or sister dies, the surviving child can carry enormous guilt. Thus, it is important that parents check to see if surviving children are experiencing survival guilt and to offer reassurance when needed.

---

[3]See Sanders, *Surviving Grief and Learning to Live Again*, p. 175, for more on children's bereavement.

Second, when parents are going through the throes of grief, it can be difficult for them to attend to the emotional needs of grieving children. Since they are suffering acute grief themselves, they will probably lack the patience, emotional resources, or functioning power to be as available to their surviving children as they have been in the past. For that reason, surviving children can feel emotionally abandoned by parents suffering from intense grief. Despite the severity of your own grief, strive to be there for your offspring, for they need your affection and love now more than ever. Your children will also benefit greatly just from your warm physical presence and from your tender explanations or answers to questions.

However, if you feel you cannot meet your children's needs, identify the limitations and get appropriate help from others. Enlist the aid of a child's teacher, a favorite relative, or a trusted friend to watch the child and to encourage healthy mourning. Even if you can't be a "super parent" at this time, you can still arrange things as much as possible so that your children's basic needs are met. Be honest with your child by letting him or her know that you are having a difficult time, too, but that you will get through it together. Try to help your child as best you can, but don't be too critical of yourself.

Third, it is not uncommon for bereaved siblings to lose a measure of their youthful innocence and joyfulness about life. The death of a brother or sister is a stark and painful reminder that life is fragile. These children may feel the weight of being a remaining or an only child, with all the implications. Tarnished and wizened at an early age, they are forever robbed of the carefree nature of their childhood.

Children can carry the scars of survival guilt, parental emotional abandonment, and lost innocence for a long time. But this is also an opportunity for a family to come together and strengthen its bonds. Young people who receive added support, reassurance, love, and a chance to talk about their feelings will be better able to handle their grief.

39. Don't Blame Yourself If Some Friendships Falter

After facing the loss of a child, it is common for parents to see a shift in their circle of friends. Our friendships may change because of personal changes we undergo after a child's death, or because of the stigma attached by others to death and grief, or because of an unrealistic timetable our friends may set for our "recovery."

You have just gone through a profound experience, so you may find that your perspective on life has changed and that your friendship needs have also changed.[4] Many friends and even relatives will not understand the adjustments you have gone through and will wish for the

---

[4]Brook Noel, *Grief Steps: 10 Steps to Regroup, Rebuild, and Renew After Any Life Loss* (Fredonia, WI: Champion Press, LTD., 2004), pp. 201-204.

return of your "old self." You have been through a tremendously difficult experience, but these friends may be unable to relate to the new person you have become.

The stigma attached to the subjects of death and grief may also propel a change in friends. Many people today seek happiness and try to avoid any painful or negative feelings. This is why some friends or relatives may be uncomfortable in expressing their condolences. The death of your child and the grief you are experiencing creates pain and sadness for them, too. Your loss has brought home to them the fact that death can happen to anyone at any time. Because the grief you are experiencing reminds them of their own family's vulnerability, some of them may avoid contact with you.

Your friends' expectations about when you should recover may also stress your friendships. They may offer directives, such as, "It's been three months, so you should be getting over it by now." Or, "You need to stop thinking about it and move on." On the other hand, friends who say "You seem to be doing better now" are eager for us to be better. A discreet response might be, "Thanks for your encouraging words, but I know I've just begun."

Keep in mind, however, that the vast majority of your friends and relatives will probably remain steadfast throughout your ordeal. In *A Grace Disguised: How the Soul Grows Through Loss*, Gerald L. Sittser writes: "grace has come to me in ways I did not expect. Friends have remained loyal and supportive in spite of my struggles."[5]

40. Don't Be Alarmed If You See Changes in Yourself

After the loss of a child, most parents perceive within themselves changes in their personal outlook on issues of life and death.[6] First, there is a sense that life has lost its innocence. Life has been shattered, like Humpty Dumpty, never to be put back together again. In addition, there can be an alteration in parents' perceptions of the control they exert over the lives of their children. In the past, before our child's death, it was comforting to suppose that we had some control over our children's safety and health. But now we know that however vigilant we may be, fate can intervene. So the sense we have as parents that life is predictable and controllable is suddenly stolen from us.

Mourning parents may notice a profound change in their notion of values and priorities. One of the shifts in values is the aspiration to be more sensitive and compassionate in regard to the needs of others. Parents become more open to the tremendous amount of suffering

---

[5]Gerald L. Sittser, *A Grace Disguised: How the Soul Grows Through Loss* (Grand Rapids: Zondervan Publishing House, 1995), p. 114.
[6]Judith R. Bernstein, *When the Bough Breaks: Forever After the Death of a Son or Daughter* (Kansas City: Andrews McMeal Publishing, 1998), pp. xv, 70-81.

in the world and acquire a new empathy for the anguish of others. Also undergoing alteration is the value placed on work, money, acquisition, and status. The transience of life causes changes in the way our priorities are ordered, so it becomes more important for us to spend quality time with loved ones than to spend time acquiring the "things" of the world. For some, materialism and greed give way to love, compassion, and gaining the most from the present moment.

Oddly, when parents lose a child, they often find themselves gaining a new sense of empowerment. Bereaved parents have been through the most horrible ordeal a parent can suffer, and yet they have survived. Because they have lived through the death of a son or daughter, the worst life could present them has already happened. No matter what life gives them now, they can handle it. Harriet Sarnoff Schiff, author of *The Bereaved Parent*, aptly summarized the idea of empowerment: "The fear of the unknown is behind us, for most of us, because we have already taken a long look at hell."[7]

A child's death is a major change in life which causes many bereaved parents to reevaluate their religious conviction. Various areas of doubts and questions are confronted in an attempt to clarify the meaning and the relevance of personal faith. Thus, the death of a child may provoke either a strengthening of faith or, conversely, a crisis of faith. Even parents who previously held strong

---

[7]Harriet Sarnoff Schiff, *The Bereaved Parent* (New York: Penguin Books, 1981), p. 144.

religious convictions may find themselves struggling with religious concepts that do not seem to match up with the sorrows of life.

Somewhere in the course of the reevaluation, however, a doubting parent may catch a renewed glimpse of faith. He or she may experience it in a golden sunrise, in the softness of a baby chick, or in the glory of a star-studded sky. Or, a parent may recognize it in acts of compassion and love bestowed during the course of bereavement. In that moment of truth, a parent may suddenly sense that something glorious and wonderful and pristine does indeed exist beyond this imperfect and painful and tarnished world in which we live.

41. Prepare Yourself to Deal With Holidays and Anniversaries

During holidays or anniversaries of important events, you will experience upsurges in grief. Some of these anniversary dates are more likely to remind you of your loved one. For instance, you may be especially saddened on the anniversary of your child's death or on his or her birthday. Other holidays such as Thanksgiving, religious celebrations, or Mother's or Father's Day are also times when you will be painfully reminded of your loss. Holidays are special occasions in our society when we are supposed to be together with loved ones. For bereaved parents, these celebrations will be painful because your child can no longer participate in festivities.[8]

Since this will be a difficult time for your entire family, ask everyone, including other children, what they would like to do on holidays. Give your plans careful thought, and don't do anything that would put you or other family members in an emotional bind. It may be a good idea to trade in old memory filled traditions and replace them with new comforting rituals. Or perhaps you might just want to alter your traditions slightly so that you don't have to highlight your loved one's absence more than it already is. For instance, you might want to have your Thanksgiving dinner or religious celebration at another relative's house instead of yours.

Keep in mind that plans for holidays can be changed from year to year. What you decide for this year can be changed next year if you want to go back to the old way. Just decide what is best for your family now and don't worry about holidays in years to come. You will be at a different place in your life in future years, so you can adapt at that time. The main concern is that you make the holidays more bearable for yourself while your grief is still fresh.

During this difficult time, consider doing something for someone else or reaching out to others, for this will bring you a measure of fulfillment and joy. When you are feeling deprived because of the loss of your child, perform

---

[8]Alan D. Wolfelt, *Healing Your Grieving Heart: 100 Practical Ideas* (Fort Collins, CO: Companion Press, 1998), pp. 40-42.

Coping with Life Changes

an act of generosity, such as donating money to a needy cause in your loved one's name or volunteering to help out in a soup kitchen. By performing kindnesses such as this, you will be acting in the true spirit of the holidays and will not only be assisting others, but will also be helping yourself.

Chapter 9

Engaging in Meaningful Activity

Although the length of the grieving process varies from parent to parent, you eventually will arrive at a bend in the road — at a gradual turning point when the seeds of renewed life will begin to take root. Relapses will recur, even when recovery is going well, because from time to time something will undoubtedly trigger a memory which brings grief flooding back in, in all its previous intensity. However, these bouts will become less frequent, will last a shorter period of time, and will become less intense.

The loss of a son or daughter requires a difficult and lengthy restructuring of identity, because our identification with our children is so strong that it may take years for us to let go of that connection.[1] But, when we let go, we are finally able to start taking pleasure in other interests and relationships.

Parents who seek and find meaningful pursuits and activities are better able to regain their sense of purpose and to revive their capacity for happiness. Renewing pleasure in your life will take courage because part of the grief of losing a child is feeling that your son or daughter was cheated of life's simple pleasures. Many parents think that giving up grief and permitting enjoyment is like stealing something that rightfully belonged to their child. To give up sadness not only feels disloyal, but it also means relinquishing a vital link to their son or daughter.

Not so. It's okay to be happy. There is a time when you should again find yourself enjoying life and pursuing new interests. Although right now you may think you will never experience real joy again, that simply is not true. Happiness is a normal human emotion, and, as time goes on, you will be able to more frequently experience that emotion.

42. Begin an Exercise Program When Your Health Improves

When your physical health is improved and your emotional state is better, you might want to begin an

---

[1] Catherine M. Sanders, *How to Survive the Loss of a Child* (New York: Three Rivers Press, 1998), p. 37.

exercise program. This will give you more energy and an improved outlook.

The exercise program you choose is up to you. The options include walking, jogging, lifting weights, cycling, or jumping rope. Body-work programs, such as polarity and reflexology or aerobic exercise, are additional excellent exercises you can do on your own. You might also want to consider team sports, such as baseball, basketball, football, soccer, volleyball, and so forth.

Another alternative is to join a health club or spa where you could receive the benefits of access to a large variety of exercise equipment and a professional staff that can provide help in areas such as fitness, strength, cardio, or motivational training. Technical instruction can also be obtained through programs such as aerobic boxing, martial arts, and aerobic dance clubs. And conventional dance studios are great places to learn square dancing, tango, swing, two-step, waltz, or the jitterbug.

Gardening and doing yard work are two other methods for getting physical exercise as well as for planting seeds of hope in your psyche. Gardening can provide a calming, healing effect because it represents the beauty and growth of nature, as well as the natural cycles of life. You might want to plant a vegetable or flower garden outside or just begin with an indoor container garden or some indoor house plants.

Or try sprucing up your home. Splash on a coat of fresh paint on your living room, or choose a cheerful wallpaper. Rearrange the furniture, hang some new drapes, or place a fresh bouquet of flowers in a prominent place. These kinds of projects will leave you feeling better not only physically but emotionally as well.

43. Volunteer Your Time or Donate Resources to Charity

At some point, you may find yourself wanting to help others. If you are still in early grief, you might want to postpone such activities, because it's best not to overload yourself too soon. But, if you are in the later stages of grief, you might want to consider volunteering your time to work at a mission, a homeless shelter, a nursing home, a Red Cross facility, or a service club.[2]

You might also be ready to reach out to help other mourners by volunteering at a hospice or by starting a support group. Many bereaved parents help out by organizing meetings, writing newsletters, and talking at length to the newly bereaved whenever they are needed. Raymond R. Mitsch and Lynn Brookside point out that

> Couples who have lost a child to crib death may choose to begin a local extension of the support group for other parents grieving the loss of children through SIDS. Mothers Against Drunk Driving (MADD) was formed by two women who had lost children in traffic accidents caused by drunk drivers. The support group

---

[2]See Judith R. Bernstein, *When the Bough Breaks: Forever After the Death of a Son or Daughter* (Kansas City: Andrews McMeal Publishing, 1998), pp. 75-76, 214-219, for more information on ways to volunteer time or donate resources.

called Parents of Murdered Children was formed by people whose pain was like no other they had ever imagined. Others who were recovering from grief and loss have chosen to become involved in hospice work and grief counseling. The list of possibilities is almost endless.[3]

Comforting other parents through support groups can be very rewarding, but one-on-one support is important, too. A phone call, a visit, a flower, a card, a hug or a word of encouragement are all important ways to connect to a parent who so desperately needs help.

The list of possibilities for things you can do is endless. What you do is not nearly as important as the fact that you are doing something, you are helping others.

If you don't have the time to volunteer, donating money or goods is another option. Make a charitable donation in your child's name. You will contribute to the welfare of others while also honoring your child's life. Scholarship funds or donations to charitable organizations such as Make-A-Wish Foundation (www.wish.org), Ronald McDonald's House (www.ronaldmcdonald.org), or St. Jude Children's Research Hospital (www.stjude.org) are excellent ways to donate in a child's name.

---

[3]Raymond R. Mitsch and Lynn Brookside, *Grieving the Loss of Someone You Love* (Ann Arbor, Michigan: Servant Publications, 1993).

44. Start an Arts and Crafts Project or a New Hobby

Crafts involve activities in which you make things with your own hands. One category of crafts involves textiles, such as cross-stitch, crocheting, dress-making, embroidery, knitting, lace-making, millinery, needlepoint, patchwork, quilting, rug-making, sewing, spinning, tapestry, tatting, and weaving.

Another category of crafts pertains to working with wood, metal, or clay. Metalworking, jewelry making, pottery, sculpture, and woodworking all fall under this category. Working with paper or canvas is another category, which includes bookbinding, calligraphy, card-making, collage, decoupage, marbling, origami, paper-mache, parchment craft, quill work, scrap booking, and stamping.

You might want to create a memory book, which contains valued momentos of the child who died. You might consider including treasured photos, school work, newspaper clippings, hair clippings, and so forth. A memory book can help you heal. A memory quilt can be another way to commemorate a life that was lived. Phone others who knew and loved your son or daughter and ask them to contribute a quilt block.

Hobbies are also a good way for grieving parents to reconnect to life. Some of the more popular hobbies include stamp or coin collecting, scale model building, bird or butterfly watching, model railroading, genealogy, and cooking. The computer is also a good source for pursuing these and other hobbies.

Reading is a hobby or activity that parents can pursue solely for entertainment or for the purpose of gaining knowledge in specific areas. When your capacity for concentration returns and when you feel ready, head to your library or bookstore to get some books. There is nothing like a good book to divert your attention from the stresses of life. The options are many: mystery novels, science fiction, romance novels, historical nonfiction, gardening books, religious or inspirational books, biographies, self-help books, cook books, or travel books.

Traveling is another hobby. A short trip or an extended vacation can restore and energize. Sometimes a change of scenery can help people see their lives from a different perspective.

Writing can also be a very therapeutic hobby. The physical act of writing can be very rewarding intellectually and emotionally. And a collection of writings can help you reflect back on how you have progressed in your grief.

45. Listen to Music or Paint

If you are interested in visual arts, you might enjoy drawing, painting, printmaking, sculpture, photography, pottery-making or ceramics. Purchase some brushes, paints, and a canvas and paint your feelings about the death, or buy some charcoal and art paper to draw your emotions. In the process, don't be concerned about your artistic abilities. Just let your imagination take charge.

Music also can be therapeutic, because it taps into the deep recesses of the emotions, both happy and sad. Most types of music can be healing. You might want to consider listening to a wide variety of music, perhaps even to music that isn't your normal fare.

If you sing or play an instrument, you would also do well to consider taking up music activities again. But if you don't have musical experience or training, it's never too late to begin. Although some people can learn to perform or improvise music without special training, many feel the need for formal lessons. This training can take the form of an apprenticeship, music lessons, or private study sessions with an individual teacher.

46. Go back to School

The loss of a child has a way of making us rethink our priorities and redefine the meaning of life. Allow yourself the chance to restructure your life around the things that truly matter to you. For example, if you want to spend more time with your family but your job consumes too much of your time, ask your boss for a reduced working schedule or, if that isn't possible, look for another job.

Alternatively, you might want to consider a new career and return to college or vocational school to train yourself for that career. If you can't take time off during the day, you might want to explore computer-based or distance educational programs.

Chapter 10

Affirming Reality

Somewhere along the path of bereavement, the burden of your load will get lighter and the pain of your loss will lessen. The changes will go unnoticed at first because they are so subtle. At some point, however, you will arrive at the beginning of your recovery.[1]

You arrive at the point where your life starts to take on purpose and meaning again. Although this process will take a long time, you will experience changes in yourself that lead to a resolution of your grief. This will occur as you come to terms with your loss, form a new identity, strengthen family relationships, and restructure your life.

---

[1] Catherine M. Sanders, *How to Survive the Loss of a Child* (New York: Three Rivers Press, 1998), p. 36.

47. Come to Terms with Your Loss

One of the characteristics of recovery involves coming to terms with your loss.[2] This happens when you have been able to process your grief to the point where you feel ready to move forward from the past. To do so, you will have to accustom yourself to the absence of your child in your life and to adapt to the lack of interaction with the son or daughter who formerly contributed so much to your world.

Moving past your grief doesn't mean that you no longer think about or miss your deceased child, for that child is a part of your life forever. But his or her role in your life must necessarily change so you can move forward.[3] Although you must relinquish the role of loving your child as you did when he or she was physically present, you can replace that with the practice of loving your absent son or daughter through your memory of them. Memories of a deceased child are priceless and ageless.

---

[2]Nancy O'Connor, *Letting Go With Love: The Grieving Process* (Tucson, AZ: La Mariposa Press, 1984), p. 27.

[3]Judith R. Bernstein, *When the Bough Breaks: Forever After the Death of a Son or Daughter* (Kansas City: Andrews McMeal Publishing, 1998), pp. 15-25.

48. Form New Identity

After you come to terms with the reality of the loss of your child, you will need to form a new identity in order to rebuild your life. Recognize that the death of your child has changed you to a large degree and that you will never be the same person you were before he or she died. You will need to develop fresh beliefs and expectations about the world without your loved one. This task will be difficult because you will undoubtedly want the world to remain the way it was before your son or daughter died. You do not want to alter your feelings about the world and the way it works.

Nevertheless, you will need to give up certain hopes, dreams, expectations, and experiences you had with your child and develop new roles, skills, behaviors, and relationships. By integrating your old and new selves together, you will be able to form a new identity.[4]

49. Move Forward in Family Relationships

The intense grief following your child's death can affect your remaining family relationships in either a positive or a negative manner.[5] Although maintaining family relationships is important, it must be remembered that relationships cannot always be mended or restored despite our very best efforts. It can seem like an almost

---

[4]Sanders, *Surviving Grief and Learning to Live Again*, p. 91.
[5]O'Connor, *Letting Go With Love*, p. vii.

unbearable double whammy if you not only lose a child through death but, then, also lose your spouse through divorce. At times, however, because misunderstandings can develop which seem insurmountable, the only option may be to accept imperfection within the marriage relationship with good grace and move forward.

Rejoice if your marriage stays intact but accept reality if your relationship with your spouse ends in divorce. Realize that you may need to eventually move past a broken marriage toward the possibility of a new healing and sustaining relationship. When the time is right for you to more actively reenter the social world, you may want to consider the possibility of dating again.[6] Church is a good place to meet new people. Dating services are also available and are a very efficient way to look for a partner.

Dating services generally require people to give personal information and to submit photographs in order to create profiles which include criteria such as age, race, gender, interests, location, religious affiliation, and so forth. Profiles are then posted so members can browse before deciding to communicate anonymously through the dating service. Members can engage in ongoing correspondence in order to get a sense of the personality, traits, and interests of another person. In this way, individuals can get to "know" one another and to better discern if someone meets their preferences in regard to

---

[6] Rando, *How to Go on Living When Someone You Love Dies*, pp. 297-299.

both practical concerns and moral standards before meeting them.

A good dating service will provide detailed, specific instructions for your safety such as advising you to refrain from giving out personal information like your name, phone number, or address in your correspondence and telling you that your first meeting should be at a restaurant or other public place. Keep in mind that you will need to be cautious and careful, because an individual may misrepresent him or herself by giving false information such as incorrect marital status, age, physical attributes or social/economic status. So be very careful. Nevertheless, the fact remains that many people have met their future spouses through dating services.

50. Restructure Your Life

At some point, you will arrive at a place where you realize that you must make a choice about recovery. The loss of your son or daughter has left an indelible imprint on your soul, and you are a substantially different person. You need to know, however, that if you choose, you can return to happiness again. Life is full of risks. But if you fail to accommodate to the changes in your life, if you persist as if the world is still the same, then you will be failing to respond to the reality of your situation.[7]

---

[7]Therese A. Rando, *How to Go on Living When Someone You Love Dies* (New York: Bantam Books, 1991), pp. 16-19.

You may be wondering what right you have to benefit from still being alive, since your child is dead. To answer that question, consider what your child would want you to do. You have suffered an incredible loss and feel guilty about moving past the loss and attempting to reunite with life. What advice on this subject would your deceased child give you if he or she could? Really think about it. Your son or daughter would encourage you to move on, to refrain from dwelling on the past, but to face the future with courage and determination. Your child wouldn't want you to remain stuck with a permanent sense of sadness or inability to progress. Moving forward is the best tribute you can pay both to life itself and to the memory of your departed child who would want you to recover.

There are some steps you can take in moving forward toward a new life. You will need to understand your feelings, formulate new answers and priorities, and restructure your life in a meaningful way so you can go on living. By successfully dealing with the changes in your life, you will not only gain a better understanding of both yourself and others, you also will achieve a higher level of growth and positive development than you ever thought possible. So, from this moment forward, live your life to the fullest.

Final Comment

Although it has been more than 25 years since my daughter Karen's death, seldom a day goes by that I do not think of her. Over the years, I have learned to say the words — "I had a daughter who died" — more calmly.

Bereaved parents are changed people. We are not the same as we were before our child's death. We are stronger and wiser, and we have more to give to others as we move past our own pain. Of course, there is also the possibility of a different outcome. There is danger that a mourning father or mother will become bitter, disillusioned, or angry about life, succumbing to fatalism and despair.

But those capable of facing loss in the knowledge that grief can be counted among the deepening experiences of life are able to count their blessings in spite of the pain they have endured. As Wolfelt explains: "You are blessed. Your life has purpose and meaning. This is not to deny the hurt, but it may help to consider the things that make your life worth living too. If you're feeling ready, make a list of the blessings in your life."[1]

For me, that list of blessings includes a deep realization of the worth of relationships, the benefits of love, the importance of lightheartedness, the significance of the present moment, and the value of faith. I hope that you, too, someday will be able to make your own list of blessings. *NSK*

---

[1] Alan D. Wolfelt, *Healing Your Grieving Heart: 100 Practical Ideas* (Fort Collins, CO: Companion Press, 1998), p. 96.

Web Site Resources

Compassionate Friends (international)
    www.compassionatefriends.org

The Bereaved Parents of the USA
    www.bereavedparentsusa.org

The Candlelighters Childhood Cancer Foundation
    www.candlelighters.org

Mothers Against Drunk Driving (MADD)
    www.madd.org

Parents of Murdered Children
    www.pomc.com

Sudden Infant Death Syndrome Support
    www.EarlyAngels.com

Pregnancy and Infant Loss Support
www.nationalshareoffice.com

Bibliography
(and for further reading)

Bernstein, Judith R. *When the Bough Breaks: Forever After the Death of a Son or Daughter.* Kansas City: Andrews McMeal Publishing, 1998.

Claypool, John. *Tracks of a Fellow Struggler.* Waco, TX: Word, 1974.

Lewis, C. S. *A Grief Observed.* New York: The Seabury Press, 1961.

Lawrenz, Mel and Green, Daniel. *Life After Grief How to Survive Loss and Trauma.* Grand Rapids: Baker Books, 1995.

Lucado, Max. *In the Eye of the Storm.* Dallas: Word, 1991.

Mitsch, Raymond R. and Brookside, Lynn. *Grieving the Loss of Someone You Love.* Ann Arbor, MI: Servant Publications, 1993.

Noel, Brook. *Grief Steps: 10 Steps to Regroup, Rebuild, and Renew After Any Life Loss*. Fredonia, WI: Champion Press, LTD., 2004.

O'Connor, Nancy. *Letting Go With Love: The Grieving Process*. Tucson, AZ: La Mariposa Press, 1984.

Rando, Therese A. *How to Go on Living When Someone You Love Dies*. New York: Bantam Books, 1991.

Salem, Harry and Salem, Cheryl. *From Grief to Glory: Rediscovering Life After Loss*. New Kensington, PA: Whitaker House, 2003.

Sanders, Catherine M. *How to Survive the Loss of a Child*. New York: Three Rivers Press, 1992.

Sanders, Catherine M. *Surviving Grief and Learning to Live Again*. New York: John Wiley and Sons, Inc., 1992.

Schiff, Harriet Sarnoff. *The Bereaved Parent*. New York: Penguin Books, 1977.

Sittser, Gerald L. *A Grace Disguised: How the Soul Grows Through Loss*. Grand Rapids: Zondervan Publishing House, 1995.

Westberg, Granger E., *Good Grief: A Constructive Approach to the Problem of Loss*. Minneapolis: Augsburg Fortress Press, 1979.

White, James R. *Grieving: Our Path Back to Peace*. Minneapolis: Bethany House Publishers, 1997.

Wolfelt, Alan D. *Healing Your Grieving Heart: 100 Practical Ideas*. Fort Collins, CO: Companion Press, 1998.

Index

A

affirming reality, 7, 17, 107
anger, 7, 17, 23, 32, 41, 42, 47, 48, 61, 65, 69-73, 75, 80, 86
anniversaries, 57, 85, 93
art, 103
ashamed, 21, 33, 40, 49, 70 (also see *shame*)

B

Bereaved Parents of the USA, 46, 47, 115
Bernstein, Judith R., 39, 40, 46, 53, 57, 58, 91, 100, 108, 117
blame, 59, 60, 63, 71, 73, 89
blessings, 113, 114
Boyles, Salynn, 83
Brookside, Lynn, 100, 101, 117

C

Candlelighters Childhood Cancer Foundation, 47, 115
charity, 100
children, 4, 13, 22, 47, 59, 62, 65, 72, 85-89, 91, 94, 97, 100, 101, 115
communicate, 62, 71, 86, 110
Compassionate Friends, 46, 47, 115
conservation, 44

D

denial, 7, 17, 19, 20, 29, 31
depression, 7, 17, 36, 39-43, 49, 71
despair, 14, 32, 34, 36, 63, 70, 113
divorce, 86, 110
donate, 100, 101

E

emotions, 7, 17, 23, 24, 28, 29, 31-33, 37, 41, 46-48, 51, 55, 65, 70, 72, 74, 80, 81, 87, 104
escape, 2, 15, 16, 20, 44, 45, 55
exercise, 42-44, 98, 99

F

faith, 16, 24, 82, 85, 92, 93, 114
family relationships, 107, 109
feelings, 11, 24, 32-36, 40-45, 48, 56, 60, 61, 65-67, 69-72, 75, 80, 86, 89, 90, 103, 109, 112
forgive yourself, 63, 64
forgiveness, 74, 75
form new identity, 109
friendships, 89, 90

G

God, 16, 25
good griever, 52
grief process, 23, 26, 31, 40, 53, 56, 81
grieving process, 16, 25, 36, 40, 42, 45, 60, 71, 78, 79, 97, 108, 118

H

health, 13, 25, 36, 41-43, 49, 77, 78, 81-83, 91, 98, 99
hobbies, 102, 103
holidays, 57, 85, 93-95

I-K

identity, 97, 107, 109
journal, 24
Koenig, Harold G., 82

L

Lawrenz, Mel, 117
lessons, 75, 104
life changes, 7, 17, 85
loneliness, 7, 17, 31, 34, 36
love, 12, 21, 22, 24, 25, 32, 36, 37, 41, 42, 44, 51, 60, 61, 69, 71, 78, 80, 86, 88, 89, 92, 93, 101, 108-111, 114, 117, 118
Lucado, Maz, 117

M

Make-A-Wish Foundation, 101
marriage, 42, 110
meaningful activity, 7, 17, 97
memory book, 102
memory quilt, 102
Mitsch, Raymond R., 100, 101, 117
Mothers Against Drunk Driving, 47, 100, 115

N-O

Noel, Brook, 54, 74, 89, 118
O'Connor, Nancy, 25, 36, 42, 44, 60, 71, 78, 80, 108, 109, 118

P

painting, 103
panic, 7, 17, 32, 51, 52, 56
parental self-reproach, 63
Parents of Murdered Children, 47, 101, 115
Pregnancy and Infant Loss Support, 47, 116
professional help, 40, 47, 48
professionals, 16, 58, 70
prolonged grief, 77

R

Rando, Therese A., 22, 24, 32, 41, 51, 61, 69, 86, 110, 111, 118
recovery, 14, 25, 37, 60, 89, 97, 107, 108, 111
Red Cross, 100
responses to change, 44
responsibilities, 21
restructure your life, 104, 107, 111, 112
revolution, 44, 45
Ronald McDonald's House, 101

S

Salem, Cheryl, 70, 82, 118
Salem, Harry, 70, 82, 118
Sanders, Catherine M., 20, 26, 41, 47, 48, 55, 63, 66, 71, 72, 77, 79, 86, 87, 98, 107, 109, 118
Schiff, Harriet Sarnoff, 92, 118
self-destruction, 37, 72
self-destructive, 48, 71-74
shame, 33
sharing, 35
shock, 7, 17, 19, 20, 26, 28, 29, 31, 32, 55
siblings, 87, 88
Sittser, Gerald L., 90, 91, 118
sleep, 13, 15, 42-44, 48
socialize, 15
sorrow, 15, 19, 23, 28, 33
St. Jude Children's Research Hospital, 101
stress, 36, 42, 43, 77, 78, 82, 90
Sudden Infant Death Syndrome Support, 47, 115
suicide, 36, 37, 54, 62-64, 71-73
Suicide Prevention Service, 37
support, 12, 14-16, 21, 22, 25, 42, 46, 47, 49, 56, 57, 64, 72, 86, 89, 100, 101, 115, 116

T-V

transcendence, 44
trust, 66, 71

unjustified guilt, 60-62
volunteer, 100, 101

W

Web MD, 83
Westberg, Granger E., 20, 31, 34, 35, 52, 118
White, James R., 33, 118
Wolfelt, Alan D., 22, 23, 28, 56, 94, 113, 114, 119